THE

PERSONAL FINANCE KIT

Ellen Norris Gruber

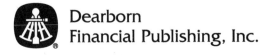
Dearborn
Financial Publishing, Inc.

This publication is designed to provide accurate and authoritative information in regard to the subject matter covered. It is sold with the understanding that the publisher is not engaged in rendering legal, accounting or other professional service. If legal advice or other expert assistance is required, the services of a competent professional person should be sought.

Managing Editor: Jack L. Kiburz
Senior Associate Editor: Karen A. Christensen
Cover Design: S. Laird Jenkins Corporation
Interior Design: Lucy Jenkins

© 1996 by Ellen Gruber

Published by Dearborn Financial Publishing, Inc.®

Printed in the United States of America

96 97 98   10 9 8 7 6 5 4 3 2

Library of Congress Cataloging-in-Publication Data

Gruber, Ellen.
    The personal finance kit / Ellen Gruber.
        p.   cm.
    Includes index.
    ISBN 0-7931-1713-5 (pbk.)
    1. Finance, Personal.   I. Title.
    HG179.G79   1996
    332.024—dc20   95-45397
                            CIP

Dearborn Financial Publishing books are available at special quantity discounts to use as premiums and sales promotions, or for use in corporate training programs. For more information, please call the Special Sales Manager at 312-621-9621, ext. 4384, or write to Dearborn Financial Publishing, Inc., 155 N. Wacker Drive, Chicago, IL 60606-1719.

Table of Contents

Preface

This kit is one of the most flexible and comprehensive personal finance workbooks on the market today. Whether you are just starting out, newly married or retiring, you will discover that this *Personal Finance Kit* is a valuable daily and lifetime reference tool.

Designed to adapt to your changing needs, *this kit's sole purpose* is to give you a well-organized and flexible way to locate and document your important financial information, to help you organize your budgets and to provide your family or caregivers easy access to important information in case of emergency.

Now, more than ever, you have a real need to be totally aware and in charge of your financial world in order to make daily financial decisions. To do this, you must be organized and prepared. By purchasing this kit and filling out the forms and worksheets listing advisers, bank accounts, credit cards, insurance, securities, taxes, wills and other assets relating to your personal finances, you are automatically organizing your personal financial life, and you will have:

- all records, investment information and any necessary receipts in one place.
- immediate access to all records in case of sudden emergency, allowing any trusted family member or friend to easily step in and take over.
- copies of all tax returns for the past seven years and know where they are.
- a workable budget and an awareness of your basic net worth—and more.

Each individually numbered form contains helpful hints and definitions. The Table of Contents positioning allows instant access to information.

For your convenience and maximum flexibility, each page has been perforated and three-hole punched. All pages that pertain to you can easily be removed from this kit and placed in an appropriate loose-leaf binder. Current statements can then be three-hole punched and inserted directly behind each relating form. Once you have organized this information in a binder, you can purchase a tab system and label it, thus ensuring immediate access to any desired section and form.

Tell every trusted adult family member, friend and adviser(s) of this book's existence. In case of need, this kit will be invaluable to anyone who must step in and take over.

Remember, this kit is for you. The forms and worksheets are simple and easy to use. Fill out only the forms, worksheets and lines that apply to your personal financial world and adapt the kit to *your* needs. Update regularly in *pencil* and keep it for life. As your assets increase, your kit will grow.

How To Use Your *Personal Finance Kit*

It is important to think of the organizational process as a gradual lifestyle change rather than a giant weekend project. As information comes to your attention, grab this kit and write it in or fill in a few forms at a time when you are paying bills or organizing taxes.

This kit has been designed for all of you, to grow with your needs throughout a lifetime. With that in mind, you may not currently relate to many of the included forms. If only a line or two applies to your needs now, don't feel compelled to complete the form. If an entire form doesn't currently apply, that's fine. Keep the form: As things change, so will the forms you need.

To keep current, try to update information as it occurs and insert current statements as they're received. It is important to *always use a pencil* so you can update information as it changes.

GETTING STARTED

1. Scan this entire kit to decide whether you want to use the kit in its current form or if you would prefer the flexibility of a loose-leaf binder.
2. If the current kit fills your needs, begin by entering all information to which you immediately relate.
3. Then, a little at a time, gather and enter related information not immediately at your fingertips. Through this process you are also organizing your personal financial records in one place.

Customizing Your Kit in a Binder

1. If a loose-leaf binder is your choice, see "What To Purchase" below.

   What To Purchase
   - An 8½″ × 11″, D-ring loose-leaf binder with an 1½″ spine, for greater expansion
   - Three sets of five blank tab packages, which you should label
   - Three-hole paper punch
   - A #10 (4⅛″ × 9½″) white envelope in which to place Form 2.1, **"In Case of Emergency"**
   - A sharp #2 pencil
   - An 8¾″ × 11¾″ white envelope in which to place appraisals and receipts for valued items. Refer to Form 8.4, **"Appraisals and Sales Receipts."**

2. Carefully remove from this kit all pages that apply to you, including the Preface, "How To Use This Kit" and the Table of Contents.
3. Insert properly labeled tabs (corresponding with the Table of Contents) and place all forms in the related tabbed sections.
4. Begin steps 2 and 3 under "Getting Started."
5. With the loose-leaf binder format, three-hole punch all applicable current original statements and place them behind each related form. If you prefer to store all original statements and documents elsewhere, photocopy the originals, place the photocopies behind the related form and indicate the location of the originals directly on the related form. Always replace with updated statements as they are received.

6. Once all forms are in place, read the instructions found at the beginning of each section pertaining to that section's forms and worksheets.

Organization brings peace of mind when you know you have all records in place for yourself and your spouse, partner, parents and heirs. By taking the time now to slowly and systematically organize your records and by filling in this kit's forms and worksheets, not only will you be taking control of your financial world today but your future as well. You will be saving time, money and later frustration.

1 Location of Documents and Records

Remember to use a pencil on all forms.

PURPOSE

It is very important for you, your spouse, your caregivers, trustee, executor or anyone who needs to step in and take over to know immediately where your important documents can be located. Refer to Form 1.1 for the list of suggested locations for storing important documents.

Form 1.2, **"Location of Documents and Records,"** is designed to:

- quickly locate important documents
- suggest how long documents should be kept
- suggest on which form in the kit information relating to a particular document can be found

HOW TO USE THESE FORMS

Refer to Form 1.2 as you begin the process of locating your documents. Start with annuity contracts. If you have such a contract, locate it, photocopy it and place the photocopy behind the related form (if you're using the loose-leaf notebook format) and store the original in a safe location. List the original document location on the worksheet. If you're using the original kit format, simply list the location of each document on the worksheet and place the document in that location.

Continue at your own pace until you have located, documented and placed the entire list of items relevant to you.

WHEN TO UPDATE

Be sure to update all information and document locations as they change.

WHEN TO TOSS

As you insert current statements, receipts and documents behind each related form, toss the outdated ones or store them in another location if you wish to keep them. If you've changed companies relating to a particular document (i.e., insurance) and no longer need the documents and statements, or if you've sold the items for which you needed the receipts, toss them. (Be sure to keep those receipts and documents after the item is sold for the recommended length of time suggested on the worksheet before tossing.)

OTHER FORMS TO KEEP

If you have documents not listed on the worksheet, write the document title on the line most closely related to the document, and list the location of the related form in the kit and the location of the original document.

1.1   Where To Keep Documents and Records

Refer to the following suggested list when storing important documents.

SAFE-DEPOSIT BOX
- Birth Certificates
- Car Title / Registration Originals
- Death Certificates
- Deeds / Mortgages
- Household inventory / Videos
- Major purchase receipts
- Marriage / Divorce papers
- Military discharge papers
- Passports
- Property appraisals
- Property improvement receipts
- Stocks / bonds / funds certificates (or with broker)

FIRE-RESISTANT BOX / SAFE

(When purchasing fire-proof safes, be sure they are guaranteed to withstand extreme heat intensities.)

- Annual pension / profit-sharing reports
- Annuities, money market, trust records
- Canceled checks for income tax
- Copies of wills
- Employment records
- Insurance policies / records
- IRA, Keogh, 401(k) records
- Lease, canceled rent and mortgage checks
- Passbooks
- Social Security cards
- Tax returns, current and past
- Warranties / Service contracts

1.2 Location of Documents and Records

This index enables you to quickly locate important documents and suggests how long they should be kept. Fill in the location of your original documents in the column headed "Location of Original."

Date Last Revised _____

Document	How Long To Keep Original	Location of Original	Location of Copy in This Book	Location of Related Form
Annuity Contracts	Life		6.9	
Adoption Papers	Life		2.2	
Advisers	Life		4	
Baptism Certificates, Birth Certificates	Life		2.2	
Business Records	Duration + 7 Years		5.2, 8.6	
Canceled Checks, Cash Account Statements	7 Years		5.1, 5.2	
Certificates of Deposit	Duration + 7 Years		5.3	
Citizenship Papers	Life		2.2	
Credit Card Index	Life		2.2, Appendix B	
Dental Records	Life, With Dentist		2.2	
Divorce, Separation Documents	Life		2.2	
Employment Contracts	Duration + 7 Years		2.2	
Final Arrangements	Life		11.3	
Burial Instructions, Plot Deed, Death Certificates	Life		11.3	
Special Bequests	Life		11.5	
Wills	Life		11.4	
Insurance Policies	Life		10	
Burial	Life		11.3	
Disability	Duration		10.2	
Disaster, Homeowner's	Duration		10.6	
Health	Life		10.1	
Income Property	Duration		10.8	
Life	Life		10.4	
Renter's	Duration		10.7	
Vehicle	Duration		10.5	
Loan, Note Agreements	Duration + 7 Years		5.4, 5.5, 9.1, 9.2	
Marriage Certificates	Life		2.2	
Medical Information, Personal	Life		2.2, 4.3	
Military Records, Service Papers	Life		2.2	
Net Worth Worksheets	Life		3.5, 3.6	
Partnership Agreements	Duration + 7 Years		8.6	

Document	How Long To Keep Original	Location of Original	Location of Copy in This Book	Location of Related Form
Limited Partnerships	Duration + 7 Years		6.8	
Passports	Life		2.2	
Personal Property			8	
Appraisals, Receipts of Valuables	Duration + 7 Years		8.2, 8.3, 8.4	
Household Inventory, Photographs, Videotapes	Life		8	
Storage Inventory, Receipts	Duration		8.1	
Durable/Health-Care Powers of Attorney	Life		11.1	
Living Will	Life		11.1	
Real Estate			9	
Appraisals, Deeds, Mortgages	Duration + 7 Years		9.1, 9.2	
Escrow Records, Title Insurance	Duration + 7 Years		9.1, 9.2	
Income Property Records	Duration + 7 Years		9.2	
Lease Documents	Duration		9.2	
Property Improvements	Duration + 7 Years		9.1, 9.2	
Retirement Plans			3.6	
IRAs, Keoghs, 401(k)s, 403(b)s	Life		7.2	
Profit-sharing	Life		7.2	
SARs, SAR/SEPTs	Life		7.2	
Stock-Option, Stock Purchase	Life		7.2	
Safe Deposit Inventory	Duration		8.1, 2.1	
Securities			6	
Annuities	Duration + 7 Years		6.9	
Bonds	Duration + 7 Years		6.4, 6.5	
Mutual Funds	Duration + 7 Years		6.6, 6.7	
Stocks	Duration + 7 Years		6.1, 6.2, 6.3	
Tax Returns	Life		12.1	
Tax-Related Canceled Checks, Receipts	7 Years		12.1	
Trust Agreements	Life		7.3	
Vehicle Title(s), Registration, Sale of	Duration + 7 Years		8.5	
Work-Related Benefits	Life		4.5, 7.2	

2 Personal Information

Remember to use a pencil on all forms.

PURPOSE

Form 2.1, **"In Case of Emergency,"** and Form 2.2, **"Family Member Information,"** have been designed to provide immediate access to your and each family member's personal and financial world. With these forms, anyone so designated can step in and easily take over in the event of an emergency situation. Here's an example: If a family member loses a wallet, simply turn to his or her form for instant credit card or driver's license numbers, or for any information you need to begin the notification process.

If an emergency arises while you and/or your spouse are away, the one in charge will have immediate access to Form 2.1, **"In Case of Emergency,"** which lists this kit's location and any relevant information needed to make decisions.

HOW TO USE THESE FORMS

Begin by filling out Form 2.1, **"In Case of Emergency."** Then, on the #10 white envelope you purchased, type or print:

| To be opened by_____ |
| Open only in case of emergency. |

Place the completed Form 2.1 in the envelope, seal and leave with the person in charge during your absence. Otherwise, always store it in your kit or binder. In addition, be certain that trusted family members or a friend or associate always know about the envelope and its location.

Next, complete Form 2.2, **"Family Member Information,"** for each family member. These forms can be helpful to have for each child as a reference even if they no longer live at home, just in case.

WHEN TO UPDATE

Be sure to update all information as it occurs. When the information listed on Form 2.1 needs updating, unseal the envelope, update the form, change envelopes and reseal, ready for use.

WHEN TO TOSS

Keep these forms for a lifetime.

OTHER FORMS TO KEEP

If you have documents or information not listed on the forms, three-hole punch and insert them in this section or indicate their location on the related form.

2.1

In Case of Emergency

Fill out this form and insert it into your #10 envelope. For detailed information about this form, refer to the first page of this section.

To My Trusted Family Member / Friend: In case of emergency, please telephone the people listed. They will take charge in my absence.

Refer to individual family member's Form 2.2 for durable health care and legal powers of attorney information.

Date Last Revised

Name

Address

E-Mail Address	WW Web Address
Phone ( )	Fax ( )
Mobile Phone ( )	Pager/Beeper ( )

Contact in Case of Emergency

Name	Phone ( )
Name	Phone ( )
Name	Phone ( )

General Information

Location of *The Personal Finance Kit*

Husband's Social Security No.	Wife's Social Security No.
Husband's Driver's License No.	Wife's Driver's License No.
Vehicle ID No.	Vehicle ID No.

Checking Account No.	Phone ( )
Financial Institution	Fax ( )

Checking Account No.	Phone ( )
Financial Institution	Fax ( )

Savings Account No.	Phone ( )
Financial Institution	Fax ( )

Location of Cash Withdrawal Slips/Enclosed

Savings Account No.

Financial Institution

Location of Cash Withdrawal Slips/Enclosed

Safe Deposit Box No.	Financial Institution

Location of Will

Location of All Credit Cards

Location of Additional Written Instructions in Case of Emergency

Other Instructions

In Case of Emergency

Continued

Attorney's Name   Mobile Phone (   )

Address

E-Mail Address   Pager/Beeper (   )

Phone (   )   Fax (   )

Accountant's Name   Mobile Phone (   )

Address

E-Mail Address   Pager/Beeper (   )

Phone (   )   Fax (   )

Auto Insurance Agent's Name   Mobile Phone (   )

Address

E-Mail Address   WW Web Address

Phone (   )   Fax (   )   Pager/Beeper (   )

Homeowner's Insurance Agent's Name   Mobile Phone

Address

E-Mail Address   WW Web Address

Phone (   )   Fax (   )   Pager/Beeper (   )

Life Insurance Agent's Name   Mobile Phone

Address

E-Mail Address   WW Web Address

Phone (   )   Fax (   )   Pager/Beeper (   )

Home Mortgage Agent's Name   Mobile Phone (   )

Address

E-Mail Address   WW Web Address

Phone (   )   Fax (   )   Pager/Beeper (   )

Primary Care Physician's Name   Mobile Phone (   )

Address

E-Mail Address   Pager/Beeper

Phone (   )   Fax (   )

Stockbroker's Name   Mobile Phone (   )

Address

E-Mail Address   WW Web Address

Phone (   )   Fax (   )   Pager/Beeper (   )

2.2

Family Member Information

Complete one form per family member. Only complete those sections or forms that pertain to you.

Date Last Revised
_____

| Name | E-Mail Address | WW Web Address |

Address _____ Mobile Phone _____

Phone ( ) _____ Fax ( ) _____

Place of Birth _____ Hospital _____

Date of Birth _____ Mother's Maiden Name _____

Social Security No. _____ Marriage Date _____

Passport No. _____ Passport Expires _____

Passport Location _____

Driver's License No. _____ Driver's License Expires _____

Auto License No. _____ Auto License Expires _____

Selective Service No. _____ Selective Service Document Location _____

To record details relating to an individual family member's insurance policies, refer to Section 10.

Describe Any Birth or Personal Identification Marks

Does This Person Wear a Medical Alert Bracelet? If So, Why?

Location of Additional Medical and Identification Information

Ex-spouse Name if Separated/Divorced

Address _____ Phone ( ) _____

Employed by

Employer's Address

Phone ( ) _____ Fax ( ) _____

E-Mail Address _____ WW Web Address _____

Is There an Employment Contract? _____ Location of Original _____

Company ID No.

Financial Institution

Type of Account _____ Account No. _____

Name(s) on Account

Access cards may include ATM, credit or debit cards. Indicate the card type and number at right. Do not include the card's PIN number.

Financial Institution Contact

Financial Institution's Address

E-Mail Address _____ WW Web Address _____

Phone ( ) _____ Fax ( ) _____

Access or ATM Card No. _____ Safe-Deposit Box? No. _____

Three-hole punch and store any relevant information after this form.

Authorized Signature(s)

Location of Records

Family Member Information

Continued

If individual family member's health adviser information differs, complete this section. If individual family member's health adviser information is the same, do not complete this form. Refer to Form 4.3.

Primary Care Physician's Name	Mobile Phone ( )
Nurse's Name	
Address	
E-Mail Address	Pager/Beeper ( )
Phone ( )	Fax ( )

Dentist's Name	Mobile Phone ( )
Assistant's or Receptionist's Name	
Address	
E-Mail Address	Pager/Beeper ( )
Phone ( )	Fax ( )

Other Health Adviser's Name	Specialty	
Address		
E-Mail Address	Mobile Phone ( )	
Phone ( )	Fax ( )	Pager/Beeper ( )

Other Health Adviser's Name	Specialty	
Address		
E-Mail Address	Mobile Phone ( )	
Phone ( )	Fax ( )	Pager/Beeper ( )

If individual family member's card number differs, complete this information. If individual family member's card numbers are the same, complete Appendix B.

Credit/Debit Card

Issued by	
Address	
Fax ( )	Lost Card Phone ( )
Card No.	Expiration Date

Issued by	
Address	
Fax ( )	Lost Card Phone ( )
Card No.	Expiration Date

Refer to Form 11.1 for definitions of Durable Health Care and Legal Powers of Attorney.

Issued by	
Address	
Fax ( )	Lost Card Phone ( )
Card No.	Expiration Date

List Who Holds Durable Health Care

List Who Holds Legal Powers of Attorney

List Designated Caretaker

List Executor of Your Estate

2.2 Family Member Information

Complete one form per family member. Only complete those sections or forms that pertain to you.

Date Last Revised

Name	E-Mail Address	WW Web Address

Address   Mobile Phone

Phone ( )   Fax ( )

Place of Birth   Hospital

Date of Birth   Mother's Maiden Name

Social Security No.   Marriage Date

Passport No.   Passport Expires

Passport Location

Driver's License No.   Driver's License Expires

Auto License No.   Auto License Expires

Selective Service No.   Selective Service Document Location

Describe Any Birth or Personal Identification Marks

Does This Person Wear a Medical Alert Bracelet? If So, Why?

Location of Additional Medical and Identification Information

Ex-spouse Name if Separated/Divorced

Address   Phone ( )

Employed by

Employer's Address

Phone ( )   Fax ( )

E-Mail Address   WW Web Address

Is There an Employment Contract?   Location of Original

Company ID No.

Financial Institution

Type of Account   Account No.

Name(s) on Account

Financial Institution Contact

Financial Institution's Address

E-Mail Address   WW Web Address

Phone ( )   Fax ( )

Access or ATM Card No.   Safe-Deposit Box?   No.

Authorized Signature(s)

Location of Records

To record details relating to an individual family member's insurance policies, refer to Section 10.

Access cards may include ATM, credit or debit cards. Indicate the card type and number at right. Do not include the card's PIN number.

Three-hole punch and store any relevant information after this form.

2.2 Family Member Information

Continued

If individual family member's health adviser information differs, complete this section. If individual family member's health adviser information is the same, do not complete this form. Refer to Form 4.3.

Primary Care Physician's Name	Mobile Phone ( )
Nurse's Name	
Address	
E-Mail Address	Pager/Beeper ( )
Phone ( )	Fax ( )
Dentist's Name	Mobile Phone ( )
Assistant's or Receptionist's Name	
Address	
E-Mail Address	Pager/Beeper ( )
Phone ( )	Fax ( )

Other Health Adviser's Name	Specialty
Address	
E-Mail Address	Mobile Phone ( )
Phone ( )	Fax ( ) Pager/Beeper ( )
Other Health Adviser's Name	Specialty
Address	
E-Mail Address	Mobile Phone ( )
Phone ( )	Fax ( ) Pager/Beeper ( )

If individual family member's card number differs, complete this information. If individual family member's card numbers are the same, complete Appendix B.

**Credit/Debit Card
Issued by**

Address

Fax (   )   Lost Card Phone (   )

Card No.   Expiration Date

Issued by

Address

Fax (   )   Lost Card Phone (   )

Card No.   Expiration Date

Refer to Form 11.1 for definitions of Durable Health Care and Legal Powers of Attorney.

Issued by

Address

Fax (   )   Lost Card Phone (   )

Card No.   Expiration Date

List Who Holds Durable Health Care

List Who Holds Legal Powers of Attorney

List Designated Caretaker

List Executor of Your Estate

3   Budgets

Remember to use a pencil on all forms.

PURPOSE

Creating a budget is the first step toward attaining a positive bottom line at month's end. Being able to face your expenditures on paper can often be traumatic. By doing so, however, you can see where to cut unnecessary expenditures and get a better grasp on your financial world.

Budgeting is a simple process, but self-control is the key to managing your money to attain your financial goals. Try to manage your spending so your expenses are always less than your income. This section provides you with two budget worksheets to help you attain a workable budget and a positive cash flow.

HOW TO USE THESE FORMS

Begin by listing your 1-year, 3-year and 5-year financial goals on Form 3.1, **"Financial Goals."** Figure how much you'll need to set aside each month to attain your goals. Enter the monthly amount you'll need to save for each item in the related box on Form 3.2, **"Creating Your Own Budget."**

Next, on Form 3.2, list all estimated income and expenses for a one-month period. At the end of the month, enter all actual income and expenses in the relating columns. Analyze all of your actual income and expenses against those estimated. Decide which changes you can make to stay within your monthly income.

Once you have determined a projected workable budget and cut unnecessary expenditures on Form 3.2, begin entering your actual monthly income and expenses on Form 3.3, **"Monthly Budget,"** and follow the instructions for that form. How do your actual income and expenses compare with your projected budget? If it could be better, return to Form 3.2 and work on your expenses. Continue this procedure until you can pat yourself on the back and show a solid positive cash flow.

It is a good idea to complete Form 3.5, **"Net Worth Worksheet,"** *after* you have gathered all other information in this kit. When complete, it will give you an accurate accounting of your total net worth. Fill out Form 3.4, **"Net Worth Worksheet at a Glance,"** each time you update Form 3.5. Soon, you will be able to see how well your financial life is progressing.

WHEN TO UPDATE

You will automatically update and evaluate your budgets as you enter income and expenses each month. Also, you will update and add to all forms in this section as information changes or is received.

WHEN TO TOSS

Toss or change outdated information as you enter new items.

OTHER FORMS TO KEEP

Other worksheets in this section include Form 3.6, **"Retirement Needs,"** and Form 3.7, **"Medical/Dental Payments Record."** You will find separate instructions on each worksheet.

Other forms in this section are *optional* but if filled out, provide an at-a-glance reference for tracking long-term expenses (such as insurance and mortgage payments). Tracking these expenses will enable you to follow increases and decreases in yearly payment amounts. Fill out all special expenses such as contributions and professional fees, which are deductible on your yearly income tax return, as you pay the bills, and refer to these expenses when filling out yearly income tax returns.

3.1 Financial Goals

List financial goals you want to achieve, such as to pay off credit cards; increase net worth; buy a new car, boat, house, or second home; pay insurance or taxes; or save for education, retirement investments and savings.

Date Last Revised _____

One Year

Name Goal	Date When Needed	Total Cost	Monthly Savings Toward Goal

Goals set a direction. You are free to change at any time.

Three Years

Name Goal	Date When Needed	Total Cost	Monthly Savings Toward Goal

Take your time. Reevaluate and restructure goals as you go along.

Five Years

Name Goal	Date When Needed	Total Cost	Monthly Savings Toward Goal

When you decide the monthly savings to apply toward your goal, work these amounts into your budget.

3.2

Instructions for Creating Your Own Budget

This form is designed to help you in the first phase of budget planning.

FIRST MONTH

When you begin creating a workable budget for your needs, start by estimating a one-month budget and enter it on Form 3.2, **"Creating Your Own Budget."** At month's end, after your expenses have been paid, enter the *actual* amounts of your income and expenses for the month also on this form.

SECOND MONTH

Once you have *estimated* and decided upon an *actual* realistic budget from the payment of your first month's expenses and have enough remaining cash to cover your everyday needs, you are ready to begin paying your second month's expenses. As you pay these expenses, enter the amounts in the related boxes on Form 3.3, **"Monthly Budget Worksheet."**

As you enter all *actual* income and expenses on Form 3.3, follow the directions on the worksheet cover to determine whether you're (+) or (−) your budget goals. At the end of your second month, if your bills total more than your income, return to Form 3.2 and rework your budget.

Continue to use Form 3.2 when re-evaluating your income and expenses. When you find your bottom line balances of income and expenses becoming lean, analyze where you can make spending cuts.

FIRST-YEAR ESTIMATE

If you would like to estimate your first year's income and expenses while creating your monthly budget, multiply your first month's *actual* income and expenses by 12 and enter the amount in the related *estimate* "Year" box on Form 3.2.

YEAR-END EVALUATION

At the end of the year, add up all of your *actual* expense and income boxes on Form 3.3, enter the totals in the related *actual* boxes on Form 3.2 and compare your *estimated* income and expense totals in Form 3.2 to your *actual* income and expense totals on 3.2. How did you do?

In addition to your monthly budget, it is important to focus on your yearly budget to understand your overall financial picture as you plan for lump-sum items, such as taxes, vacations and holiday gifts. It also helps you to see where changes can be made as you begin your second year of budgeting.

3.2 Creating Your Own Budget

Enter all *estimated* and *actual* income for one month below. Also include *estimated* monthly and *actual* expenses.

This form is for budget estimate calculations only.

Income		Month		Year	
		$ Estimate	$ Actual	$ Estimate	$ Actual
	Wages				
	Outside Income				
	Dividends				
	Interest				
	Rent				
	Trusts				
	Investments				
	Alimony/Child Support				
	Loans Owed to You				
	Bonuses				
	Retirement				
	Government Income				
	Other				
	Total Income		$		$
Outgo of Set Expenses					
Taxes	Social Security				
	Federal, State, Local				
	Real Estate				
	Other				
Insurance	Automobile				
	Homeowner's				
	Life				
	Health/Disability				
	Long-Term Care				
	Other				
Home Operation	Mortgage/Rent				
	Outside Maintenance				
	Inside Maintenance				
	Improvements				
	Condo Fees				
	Electricity/Gas				
	Phone				
	Water/Sewer				
	Other				
	Total Set Expenses		$		$

Include monthly installment and credit card expenses in related category.

Creating Your Own Budget

Continued

		Month		Year	
Outgo of Flexible Expenses		$ Estimate	$ Actual	$ Estimate	$ Actual
Family Maintenance	Food				
	Clothing				
	Health Costs				
	Child Day Care				
	Tuition/Lessons				
	Weekend Sitters				
	Books/Supplies				
	Personal Care				
	Allowances				
	Dry Cleaning				
	Other				
Automobile Transportation	Gas/Wash				
	Repair				
	Parking/Transit/Tolls				
	License				
	Recreational Vehicle				
	Other				
Discretionary	Entertainment				
	Travel/Vacations				
	Hobbies				
	Contributions				
	Gifts				
	Lunch (Work)				
	Other				
Miscellaneous	Fees/Dues				
	Alimony				
	Dependent Support				
	Savings/Investments				
	Other				
Total Actual Flexible Expenses		$		$	
Total Actual Set + Flexible Expenses		$		$	

Net Cash Balance

	Month		Year	
Total Income	$		$	
(–) Total All Expenses	$		$	
(=) Total Remaining Cash	$		$	

If your total remaining cash is positive, you have established a workable budget.

To calculate budget totals, subtract total expenses from total income.

Once this form is complete, decide which changes can be made to stay within your budget.

Analyze totals between expenses and income. If expenses exceed income, decide where to cut expenses.

3.3 Instructions for Completing the Monthly Budget Worksheet

This form is designed to be used once you have set your budget from Form 3.2, "Creating Your Own Budget."

Budgeting is a simple process. The key is to manage your spending so your expenses are always less than your income.

By entering your *actual* income and expenses on Form 3.3, **"Monthly Budget,"** as you pay your monthly expenses, you will be able to assess your financial position, change your spending patterns and attain your financial goals.

FIRST OF THE MONTH

At the beginning of each month, enter your *actual* budget *expenses* from Form 3.2 in the related "Monthly Budget Goal" box.

END OF THE MONTH

At the end of each month, total all income and expenses of each category for the month, and enter the totals in the related boxes on Form 3.3. Subtract your monthly expenses from your monthly income, as shown, and enter the amount in the "Total Remaining Net Cash" box. Compare actual "Total Remaining Net Cash" to "Budget Goals" and indicate whether you are (+) or (−) of your goal in the appropriate box.

BUDGET EVALUATION

If you are (−) your goal, refer to Form 3.2, **"Creating Your Own Budget,"** for a budget reevaluation.

3.3 Monthly Budget

Once a workable budget is in place, begin entering actual income and expenses here.

Year _____

Income		Jan	Feb	March	April	May	June	July	Aug	Sept	Oct	Nov	Dec
	Wages												
	Outside Income												
	Dividends												
	Interest												
	Rent												
	Trusts												
	Investments												
	Alimony/Child Support												
	Loans Owed to You												
	Bonuses												
	Retirement												
	Government Income												
	Other												
	Total Income	$	$	$	$	$	$	$	$	$	$	$	$

Outgo of Set Expenses

		Jan	Feb	March	April	May	June	July	Aug	Sept	Oct	Nov	Dec
Taxes	Social Security												
	Federal/State/Local												
	Real Estate												
	Other												
Insurance	Automobile												
	Homeowner's												
	Life												
	Health/Disability												
	Long-Term Care												
	Other												
Home Operation	Mortgage/Rent												
	Outside Maintenance												
	Inside Maintenance												
	Improvements												
	Condo Fees												
	Electricity/Gas												
	Phone												
	Water/Sewer												
	Other												
	Total Set Expenses	$	$	$	$	$	$	$	$	$	$	$	$

Include monthly install-ment and credit card expenses in related category.

As you pay bills each month, place totals of income and outgo in the related column.

Refer to Form 1.2 for location of all canceled checks.

Outgo of Flexible Expenses		Jan	Feb	March	April	May	June	July	Aug	Sept	Oct	Nov	Dec
Family Maintenance	Food												
	Clothing												
	Health Costs												
	Child Day Care												
	Tuition/Lessons												
	Weekend Sitters												
	Books/Supplies												
	Personal Care												
	Allowances												
	Dry Cleaning												
	Other												
Automobile Transportation	Gas/Wash												
	Repair												
	Parking/Transit/Tolls												
	License												
	Recreational Vehicle												
	Other												
Discretionary	Entertainment												
	Travel/Vacations												
	Hobbies												
	Contributions												
	Gifts												
	Lunch (Work)												
	Other												
Miscellaneous	Fees/Dues												
	Alimony												
	Dependent Support												
	Savings/Investments												
	Other												
Total Flexible Expenses		$	$	$	$	$	$	$	$	$	$	$	$
Total Expenses (Set + Flexible)													
Total Income													
(–) Total Expenses													
(=) Total Remaining Net Cash													
Monthly Budget Goal													
(+) or (–) Goal													

Always try to pay yourself first before paying bills.

Set a reasonable budget, stay within it and you should always have more control of your money.

3.4

Net Worth Worksheet at a Glance

Enter the current date and your net worth for that date below before updating all net worth facts. Repeat this each time you update. This will provide a long-term record of how you are doing.

Date	Net Worth before Revision
	$
	$
	$
	$
	$
	$
	$
	$
	$
	$
	$
	$
	$
	$
	$
	$
	$
	$
	$
	$
	$
	$
	$
	$
	$
	$
	$
	$
	$
	$

Net Worth Worksheet

You can calculate asset totals on this worksheet by referring to the related form number listed below. Update this once each year or whenever you have a major change in your financial life.

Date Last Revised

Assets	Form Number	Amount
Current Assets		
Bonuses or Commissions	3.2, 3.3	$
Cash Accounts	5.1	$
Certificates of Deposits	5.3	$
Savings Bonds	6.4	$
Tax Refunds	12.1	$
Treasury Bills	6.4, 6.5	$
Cash Value in Life Insurance	10.4	$
Personal Securities		
Bonds	6.4, 6.5	$
Limited Partnerships	6.8	$
Mutual Funds	6.6, 6.7	$
Stocks	6.1, 6.2	$
Real Estate		
Mortgages Owned	3.10, 5.5, 9.1	$
Residence	9.1	$
Income Property	9.2	$
Secondary Residence	9.1	$
Retirement Funds		
Annuities	6.9	$
IRAs	7.2	$
Keogh Accounts	7.2	$
Pension Plans	7.2	$
Personal Property		
Business Owned	5.2, 8.6	$
Hard Assets	8.3	$
Personal Property	8.1, 8.2, 8.3	$
Vehicles	8.5	$
Other Assets		
		$
		$
		$
		$
Total Assets		$

Cash accounts are checking, savings or money market funds.

An *asset* is anything owned.

3.5

Net Worth Worksheet

Continued

This completed and updated form is helpful when applying for a loan.

Liabilities	Form Number	Amount
Current Liabilities		
Alimony	3.2, 3.3	$
Child Support	3.2, 3.3	$
Loans to Individuals	5.4	$
Unpaid Taxes		
Income Tax	12.1	$
Capital Gains Tax	12.1	$
Property Tax	3.11, 9.1	$
Real Estate Liabilities		
Residence	9.1	$
Income Property	9.2	$
Secondary Residence	9.1	$
Installment Liabilities		
Vehicle Loans/Recreational Vehicles	5.4	$
Bank/Finance Loans	5.4	$
Credit Card Charges	5.4	$
Educational Loans	5.4	$
Furniture	5.4	$
Home Improvement	5.4	$
Life Insurance Loans	10.4	$
Pension Plan Loans	7.2	$
Other Liabilities		
		$
		$
		$
		$
		$
		$
Total Liabilities		$
Total Assets		$
Total Liabilities		− $
Total Net Worth		= $

Include second mortgages.

A liability *is anything owed to an institution, company or individual.*

To calculate your net worth, simply subtract total liabilities from total assets.

3.6

Retirement Needs

Fill out the charts below *after* you have completed all forms in this kit. Completed forms can be used as references.

Once this form is complete, it should give you a rough estimate of where you are now and what you need for your future security.

Helpful Hint
A very conservative estimate of total income needed in retirement is 80% to 100% of your current salaried expenses.

Date Last Revised _____

Projected Yearly Retirement Income	Your Yearly Income	Spouse's Yearly Income	Total Yearly Income
IRA funds			
Savings (All)			
Investments (All)			
Insurance Settlements			
Annual Pension Benefits			
Annual Social Security Benefits			
Retirement Part-Time Work			
Income Other Sources			

Refer to all related forms for total retirement amounts.

Total Retirement Income $

Current Yearly Expenses	Your Expenses	Spouse's Expenses	Total Expenses
Include all expenses	$	$	$

Refer to Form 3.3, "Monthly Budgets," for your current yearly expenses.

Net Projected Yearly Retirement Cash Available after Expenses

Remaining Retirement Cash: Retirement Income (–) Current Expenses = $

For Information on Social Security benefits due you, write or call:

Social Security Administration
P.O. Box 17743
Baltimore, MD 21235
800-772-1213
Form SSA-7004-PC

Compare total yearly retirement income with 80% to 100% of your current yearly expenses. If your retirement doesn't look workable here or if you are not showing solid remaining cash, reconsider your retirement investments and where you can make changes.

Notes: _____

_____

_____

Remember, this is only a rough estimate.

To figure approximate annual income from retirement funds, divide the number of years you expect to need retirement income into the total amount in each retirement fund.

3.7 Medical / Dental Payment Record

As insurance forms are submitted and doctors are paid, enter information below. Helps track payments, dates paid and total amount of own money spent for IRS filing. Begin a new worksheet each year.

Year _____

Pretax Amount Paid To You	Deductible Satisfied? Yes	No	Co-Pay Amt. Paid	Name of Family Member/Dr.	Date of Visit	Amt. of Chg.	Date Bill To Insur.	Sent by Whom	Amt. Insur. Paid	Date Insur. Paid	Date Dr. Paid	$ Paid out of Pocket	Approx. Mileage

$ _____ Subtotal $ _____ Subtotal $ _____ Subtotal $ _____ Subtotal $ _____ Subtotal

To list additional and total charges this year, continue on the back of this page.

Pretax Amount Paid To You	Deductible Satisfied? Yes	No	Co-Pay Amt. Paid	Name of Family Member/Dr.	Date of Visit	Amt. of Chg.	Date Bill To Insur.	Sent by Whom	Amt. Insur. Paid	Date Insur. Paid	Date Dr. Paid	$ Paid out of Pocket	Approx. Mileage

$ _____ **Subtotal** $ _____ **Subtotal** $ _____ **Subtotal** $ _____ **Subtotal** $ _____ **Subtotal**

_____ **$ Total**   _____ **$ Total**   _____ **$ Total**   _____ **$ Total**   _____ **$ Total**

Location of all bills and records _____

_____

_____

3.8

Vehicle Maintenance

List all repairs and tire purchases for future at-a-glance reference.

Vehicle Year _____ Model/Make _____

Repair Company _____

Mechanic's Name _____

Address _____

Phone (   ) _____ Fax (   ) _____

Major Repairs

Date	Odometer Reading	Service Repair	Under Warranty?	$ Cost

Location of all service / repair records _____

Refer to Form 8.5, "Vehicles Owned," for detailed information regarding individual vehicles.

Helpful Hint
Be sure to check service manual for all suggested maintenance dates.

See reverse side for tire purchase dates and related information.

Vehicle Maintenance

Continued

Auto Repairs

Date	Odometer Reading	Service Repair	Under Warranty?	$ Cost

Tire Purchase

Where Purchased

Address

Phone (   )   Fax (   )

Date	Odometer Reading	Which Tires Replaced?	Guaranteed Mileage	Tire Cost	Date of Realignment

Helpful Hint
Timely realignment pro-
longs the life of the tire.

Location of all tire purchase records _____

3.9

Vehicle License Tax Tracking

List all automobiles, boats, mobile homes, motorcycles, etc., for which you pay registration fees.

Vehicle 1

Vehicle Model/Make	Vehicle Year	Check Number	Date Paid	$ Amount Paid

Vehicle 2

Refer to Form 8.5, "Vehicles Owned," for detailed vehicle information.

Vehicle Model/Make	Vehicle Year	Check Number	Date Paid	$ Amount Paid

Location of current registration forms _____

_____

_____

Store all receipts, as received, in an accessible place. That way, they'll be readily accessible during income tax preparation and for future reference.

At present, vehicle license taxes can be deducted on both your federal and state income tax returns.

Vehicle License Tax Tracking

Continued

Vehicle 3

Vehicle Model/Make	Vehicle Year	Check Number	Date Paid	$ Amount Paid

Vehicle 4

Vehicle Model/Make	Vehicle Year	Check Number	Date Paid	$ Amount Paid

3.10

Mortgage Payment Tracking

Fill in mortgage payment totals and amount owed at year end. This will help track amount paid and owed for at-a-glance reference over the life of the loan.

Date Last Revised _____

| Mortgage Lender | Contact |

Address

| Phone ( ) | Mobile Phone ( ) | Pager/Beeper ( ) |

| E-Mail Address | WW Web Address |

| Original Loan Amount $ | Refinance Loan Amount $ | Ref. Date |

| Type of Loan | Monthly Payment $ |

| Original Interest % | Refinance Interest % |

Year-End Date	Total Yearly Payment	Amount Owed Year-End

For additional property details, refer to Form 9.1, "Residence."

If you refinance, draw a red line under the year-end date of the year the refinance occurred.

For Property Tax Tracking, on this property, see reverse side.

3.11   Property Tax/City Tax Tracking

Fill in one row per year for your property tax biannual payments. Also fill in your yearly city tax payments. This will help you track tax amounts paid over the life of your property ownership.

Property Tax

Property Address _____

	Date Paid	$ Amount Paid	Date Paid	$ Amount Paid	Yearly Total
1.					
2.					
3.					
4.					
5.					
6.					
7.					
8.					
9.					
10.					
11.					
12.					
13.					
14.					
15.					
16.					
17.					
18.					
19.					
20.					

Usually, property taxes are paid biannually.

City Tax

	Date of Year Paid	$ Amount Paid		Date of Year Paid	$ Amount Paid
1.			9.		
2.			10.		
3.			11.		
4.			12.		
5.			13.		
6.			14.		
7.			15.		
8.			16.		

Usually, city taxes are paid one time each year.

3.12 Yearly Interest Paid Summary

This form is helpful for at-a-glance reference. Include all interest paid to financial institutions and other sources that must be reported on IRS statements.

Year _____

Paid To Whom	Date Quarterly				Amount $ Quarterly				Total $ Paid

Total Interest Paid $ _____

Location of all statements and receipts _____

_____

_____

Store all quarterly and year-end interest paid statements in an accessible place as received. That way, they'll be readily accessible during income tax preparation and for future reference.

3.13 Professional/Miscellaneous Fees

As fees are paid, record information in the relating section below. Total at year-end for easy reference.

Year _____

Income Tax Preparation Fee
Accounting Fees

Name	Business Expense? Yes	No	% to Bus.	Check Number	Date Paid	$ Amount Paid

Total Paid $ _____

Legal Fees

Name	Business Expense? Yes	No	% to Bus.	Check Number	Date Paid	$ Amount Paid

Total Paid $ _____

Store all fees and receipts in an accessible place as received. That way, they'll be readily accessible during income tax preparation and for future reference.

Safe-Deposit Box Fees

Name	Business Expense? Yes	No	% to Bus.	Check Number	Date Paid	$ Amount Paid

Total Paid $ _____

Other Fees

Name	Business Expense? Yes	No	% to Bus.	Check Number	Date Paid	$ Amount Paid

Total Paid $ _____

Location of all canceled checks and receipts _____

3.14　Charitable Donations

List all cash and noncash contributions made during the year. For all donations keep evidence of substantiation. Begin a new worksheet each year.

Year _____

Cash Contributions

To Whom Contributed	Cash?	Check Number	Date Paid	$ Amount Paid
			Total $	

Noncash Contributions

To Whom Contributed	Description	Date Contributed	Valued Amount
		Total $	

Store all donation receipts in an accessible place as received. That way, they'll be readily accessible during income tax preparation and for future reference.

Location of all canceled checks and receipts _____

_____

3.15 Dividend / Interest Income

This form is helpful for at-a-glance reference. Include income from all securities, financial institution accounts, limited partnerships, loans and any other sources.

Year _____

Received From Whom	Date Quarterly				Amount $ Quarterly				Total $ Received

Total Interest Income $ _____

Location of all statements and receipts _____

_____

Store all quarterly and year-end interest paid statements in an accessible place as received. That way, they'll be readily accessible during income tax preparation and for future reference.

4 Advisers

Remember to use a pencil on all forms.

PURPOSE

It is extremely important that you find good advisers with whom you can work and whom you trust. You have a lot at stake—you're placing yourself and your family in their hands.

Asking questions of them, before you decide to retain their services, will reduce costly mistakes.

Be sure to ask:

- Do they solely rely on income or is part of their income from sales commissions? If partly commissions, look elsewhere. You need an adviser, not a salesperson.
- How long have they been working in this capacity? Less then three years doesn't show enough experience.
- Can they provide a fee schedule?
- What is their educational experience?
- Can they give references? Ask all references the adviser's strengths and weaknesses.
- Do they provide written strategies and recommendations?

The forms in this section are designed to list one or all of your advisers. By doing so, they will provide you, your family, executor or caregiver instant access to this important information.

HOW TO USE THESE FORMS

Even if you have only one adviser, fill in the forms or lines to which you relate. Save the others for future use.

WHEN TO UPDATE

Be sure to update all information and changes as they occur. When you acquire a new adviser, be sure to list him or her on the proper form.

WHEN TO TOSS

These forms are intended to be kept for your lifetime.

OTHER FORMS TO KEEP

If you have documents or information not listed on the forms, three-hole punch and insert them in this section or indicate their location on the appropriate form.

4.1 Financial Advisers

Complete only those sections or forms that pertain to you.

Helpful Hint
Give a photocopy of this form to persons who should have the information in case of emergency. Some examples include adult children, your attorney, executor, trustee or someone holding your power of attorney.

Date Last Revised

Accountant's Name

Assistant's Name	Copy of Tax Forms in Office?
Firm's Name	
Firm's Address	
E-Mail Address	WW Web Address
Phone ( )	Mobile Phone ( )
Fax ( )	Pager/Beeper ( )

Financial Planner's Name

Assistant's Name	Copy of Tax Forms in Office?
Firm's Name	
Firm's Address	
E-Mail Address	WW Web Address
Phone ( )	Mobile Phone ( )
Fax ( )	Pager/Beeper ( )

Banker's Name

Institution's Name	
Institution's Address	
E-Mail Address	WW Web Address
Phone ( )	Mobile Phone ( )
Fax ( )	Pager/Beeper ( )

Securities Broker's Name

Assistant's Name	
Institution's Name	
Institution's Address	
E-Mail Address	WW Web Address
Phone ( )	Mobile Phone ( )
Fax ( )	Pager/Beeper ( )
Type of Account	Account No.

Three-hole punch and store any relevant information after this form.

Securities Broker's Name

Assistant's Name

Institution's Name

Institution's Address

E-Mail Address	WW Web Address
Phone ( )	Mobile Phone ( )
Fax ( )	Pager/Beeper ( )
Type of Account	Account No.

Other	Specialty

Assistant's Name

Firm's Name

Firm's Address

E-Mail Address	WW Web Address
Phone ( )	Mobile Phone ( )
Fax ( )	Pager/Beeper ( )
Type of Account	Account No.

Other	Specialty

Assistant's Name

Firm's Name

Firm's Address

E-Mail Address	WW Web Address
Phone ( )	Mobile Phone ( )
Fax ( )	Pager/Beeper ( )
Type of Account	Account No.

Three-hole punch and store any relevant information after this form.

4.2   Legal Advisers

Complete only those sections or forms that pertain to you.

Date Last Revised

Attorney's Name	Specialty
Assistant or Paralegal's Name	Copy of Wills in Office?
Firm's Name	
Firm's Address	
E-Mail Address	
Phone ( )	Mobile Phone ( )
Fax ( )	Pager/Beeper ( )
Attorney's Name	Specialty
Assistant or Paralegal's Name	Copy of Wills in Office?
Firm's Name	
Firm's Address	
E-Mail Address	
Phone ( )	Mobile Phone ( )
Fax ( )	Pager/Beeper ( )
Attorney's Name	Specialty
Assistant or Paralegal's Name	Copy of Wills in Office?
Firm's Name	
Firm's Address	
E-Mail Address	
Phone ( )	Mobile Phone ( )
Fax ( )	Pager/Beeper ( )
Attorney's Name	Specialty
Assistant or Paralegal's Name	Copy of Wills in Office?
Firm's Name	
Firm's Address	
E-Mail Address	
Phone ( )	Mobile Phone ( )
Fax ( )	Pager/Beeper ( )

Helpful Hint
Give a photocopy of this form to persons who should have the information in case of emergency. Some examples include adult children, your attorney, executor, trustee or someone holding your power of attorney.

Three-hole punch and store any relevant information after this form.

Other | Specialty

Assistant or Paralegal's Name | Copy of Wills in Office?

Firm's Name

Firm's Address

E-Mail Address

Phone ( ) | Mobile Phone ( )

Fax ( ) | Pager/Beeper ( )

Other | Specialty

Assistant or Paralegal's Name | Copy of Wills in Office?

Firm's Name

Firm's Address

E-Mail Address

Phone ( ) | Mobile Phone ( )

Fax ( ) | Pager/Beeper ( )

Other | Specialty

Assistant or Paralegal's Name | Copy of Wills in Office?

Firm's Name

Firm's Address

E-Mail Address

Phone ( ) | Mobile Phone ( )

Fax ( ) | Pager/Beeper ( )

Other | Specialty

Assistant or Paralegal's Name | Copy of Wills in Office?

Firm's Name

Firm's Address

E-Mail Address

Phone ( ) | Mobile Phone ( )

Fax ( ) | Pager/Beeper ( )

Three-hole punch and store any relevant information after this form.

4.3

Health Advisers

Complete only those sections or forms that pertain to you.

For insurance policy information, refer to Section 10.

If individual family member's health adviser information is the same, complete this form. If individual family member's health adviser information differs, do not complete this form. Refer to Form 2.2, "Family Member Information."

Helpful Hint
If you move or change doctors, dentists or other health advisers, have all records forwarded. This helps to avoid duplication of x-rays and tests. Complete medical histories can be crucial to proper diagnosis and treatment.

Three-hole punch and store any relevant information after this form.

Date Last Revised

Primary Care Physician's Name — Specialty

Nurse's Name

Address — Suite No.

E-Mail Address — Fax (   )

Phone (   ) — Emergency Phone (   )

Mobile Phone (   ) — Pager/Beeper (   )

Other Physician's Name — Specialty

Nurse's Name

Address — Suite No.

E-Mail Address — Fax (   )

Phone (   ) — Emergency Phone (   )

Mobile Phone (   ) — Pager/Beeper (   )

Other — Specialty

Nurse's Name

Address — Suite No.

E-Mail Address — Fax (   )

Phone (   ) — Emergency Phone (   )

Mobile Phone (   ) — Pager/Beeper (   )

Hospital/Clinic — Medical Records No.

Attending Physician's Name — Nurse's Name

Address — Suite No.

E-Mail Address — Fax (   )

Phone (   ) — Emergency Phone (   )

Mobile Phone (   ) — Pager/Beeper (   )

Location in Household of Complete Medical Information for Each Family Member

Dentist's Name

Assistant/Receptionist's Name

Address   Suite No.

E-Mail Address   Fax (   )

Phone (   )   Emergency Phone (   )

Mobile Phone (   )   Pager/Beeper (   )

Orthodontist's Name

Assistant/Receptionist's Name

Address   Suite No.

E-Mail Address   Fax (   )

Phone (   )   Emergency Phone (   )

Mobile Phone (   )   Pager/Beeper (   )

Periodontist's Name

Assistant/Receptionist's Name

Address   Suite No.

E-Mail Address   Fax (   )

Phone (   )   Emergency Phone (   )

Mobile Phone (   )   Pager/Beeper (   )

Other   Specialty

Assistant/Receptionist's Name

Address   Suite No.

E-Mail Address   Fax (   )

Phone (   )   Emergency Phone (   )

Mobile Phone (   )   Pager/Beeper (   )

Other   Specialty

Assistant/Receptionist's Name

Address   Suite No.

E-Mail Address   Fax (   )

Phone (   )   Emergency Phone (   )

Mobile Phone (   )   Pager/Beeper (   )

Three-hole punch and store any relevant information after this form.

4.4

Insurance Advisers

Complete only those sections or forms that pertain to you.

For information about
specific policies, refer to
Section 10.

Date Last Revised

Health Insurance Agent's Name

Assistant's Name	Pager/Beeper ( )
Agent's Company	Mobile Phone ( )
Address	
E-Mail Address	WW Web Address
Phone ( )	Fax ( )

Health Insurance Agent's Name

Assistant's Name	Pager/Beeper ( )
Agent's Company	Mobile Phone ( )
Address	
E-Mail Address	WW Web Address
Phone ( )	Fax ( )

Life Insurance Agent's Name

Assistant's Name	Pager/Beeper ( )
Agent's Company	Mobile Phone ( )
Address	
E-Mail Address	WW Web Address
Phone ( )	Fax ( )

Life Insurance Agent's Name

Assistant's Name	Pager/Beeper ( )
Agent's Company	Mobile Phone ( )
Address	
E-Mail Address	WW Web Address
Phone ( )	Fax ( )

Other Insurance Adviser's Name — Specialty

Assistant's Name	Pager/Beeper ( )
Agent's Company	Mobile Phone ( )
Address	
E-Mail Address	WW Web Address
Phone ( )	Fax ( )

Three-hole punch and
store any relevant
information after this form.

Insurance Advisers

Continued

Property/Casualty Agent's Name

Assistant's Name

Pager/Beeper (   )

Agent's Company

Mobile Phone (   )

Address

E-Mail Address

WW Web Address

Phone (   )

Fax (   )

Property Address

Property/Casualty Agent's Name

Assistant's Name

Pager/Beeper (   )

Agent's Company

Mobile Phone (   )

Address

E-Mail Address

WW Web Address

Phone (   )

Fax (   )

Property Address

Vehicle Insurance Agent's Name

Assistant's Name

Pager/Beeper (   )

Agent's Company

Mobile Phone (   )

Address

E-Mail Address

WW Web Address

Phone (   )

Fax (   )

Vehicle(s) Insured

Vehicle Insurance Agent's Name

Assistant's Name

Pager/Beeper (   )

Agent's Company

Mobile Phone (   )

Address

E-Mail Address

WW Web Address

Phone (   )

Fax (   )

Vehicle(s) Insured

Three-hole punch and store any relevant information after this form.

4.5

Other Advisers

Complete only those sections or forms that pertain to you.

For information about specific policies, refer to Section 10.

Date Last Revised

Executor/Trustee's Name

Assistant's Name	Pager/Beeper ( )
Address	Mobile Phone ( )
E-Mail Address	WW Web Address
Home Phone ( )	Mobile Phone ( )
Work Phone ( )	Fax ( )
Copy of Wills in Office?	Copy of Tax Forms in Office?

Work-Related Benefits Counselor's Name

Assistant's Name	Pager/Beeper ( )
Address	Mobile Phone ( )
E-Mail Address	WW Web Address
Phone ( )	Fax ( )

Work-Related Benefits Counselor's Name

Assistant's Name	Pager/Beeper ( )
Address	Mobile Phone ( )
E-Mail Address	WW Web Address
Phone ( )	Fax ( )

Mortgage Broker/Lender's Name

Assistant's Name	Account No.
Company Name	Pager/Beeper ( )
Address	Mobile Phone ( )
E-Mail Address	WW Web Address
Phone ( )	Fax ( )
Property Address	

Mortgage Broker/Lender's Name

Assistant's Name	Account No.
Company Name	Pager/Beeper ( )
Address	Mobile Phone ( )
E-Mail Address	WW Web Address
Phone ( )	Fax ( )
Property Address	

Three-hole punch and store any relevant information after this form.

Real Estate Agent's Name	Specialty
Assistant's Name	Pager/Beeper ( )
Company Name	Mobile Phone ( )
Address	
E-Mail Address	WW Web Address
Phone ( )	Fax ( )
Real Estate Agent's Name	Specialty
Assistant's Name	Pager/Beeper ( )
Company Name	Mobile Phone ( )
Address	
E-Mail Address	WW Web Address
Phone ( )	Fax ( )
Religious/Spiritual Adviser's Name	
Address	
Mobile Phone ( )	Pager/Beeper ( )
E-Mail Address	WW Web Address
Phone ( )	Fax ( )
Other	Specialty
Company Name	
Address	
Mobile Phone ( )	Pager/Beeper ( )
E-Mail Address	WW Web Address
Phone ( )	Fax ( )
Other	Specialty
Company Name	
Address	
Mobile Phone ( )	Pager/Beeper ( )
E-Mail Address	WW Web Address
Phone ( )	Fax ( )

Three-hole punch and store any relevant information after this form.

5   Banking

Remember to use a pencil on all forms.

PURPOSE

Today, an individual can "bank" at many types of financial institutions: banks, savings and loans and brokerage companies. One can "bank" by phone and computer.

It is important to compare offered services and fees charged, and then choose the best financial institution that suits your individual needs.

This section provides forms on which to list all financial institutions where you hold personal and business accounts. Also, it provides forms on which to list information regarding **Certificates of Deposit,** and **Loans and Mortgages Owed** and **Owned** for instant access.

HOW TO USE THESE FORMS

Fill out the forms or lines that apply to you. If you have only one account, that's fine. Keep the other forms for future use as your financial life changes.

WHEN TO UPDATE

Be sure to update information as it occurs. As you acquire new accounts, loans or mortgages, list them in this section.

WHEN TO TOSS

These forms are intended for you to keep for a lifetime.

OTHER FORMS TO KEEP

If you have documents or information not listed on the forms, three-hole punch and insert them in this section.

5.1

Cash Accounts

If you have several accounts with one bank, it is unnecessary to repeat common information for each account. Complete only those sections or forms that pertain to you.

Date Last Revised

Cash Accounts Held

Financial Institution

Type of Account   Account No.

Name(s) on Account

Address

E-Mail Address   WW Web Address

A *cash account* is defined as an account that may be accessed immediately and is held at one of the following institutions: bank, savings and loan, credit union or investment brokerage.

Contact

Phone (   )   Fax (   )

Access/ATM Card No.   Affiliated ATM Card Systems

Location of Checks/Book

Authorized Signature(s)

Financial Institution

Type of Account   Account No.

Name(s) on Account

Address

Helpful Hint

When total deposits in one financial institution approach $100,000, check to see if you still qualify for federal deposit insurance. If not, you may want to consider an additional and separate account in a different institution to keep all money federally insured

E-Mail Address   WW Web Address

Contact

Phone (   )   Fax (   )

Access/ATM Card No.   Affiliated ATM Card Systems

Location of Checks/Book

Authorized Signature(s)

Financial Institution

Type of Account   Account No.

Name(s) on Account

Address

E-Mail Address   WW Web Address

Access cards may include ATM, credit or debit cards. Indicate the card type and number. Do not indicate the PIN number.

Contact

Phone (   )   Fax (   )

Access/ATM Card No.   Affiliated ATM Card Systems

Location of Checks/Book

Authorized Signature(s)

Three-hole punch and store any relevant information after this form.

Cash Accounts

Continued

Financial Institution

Type of Account _____ Account No. _____

Name(s) on Account _____

Address _____

E-Mail Address _____ WW Web Address _____

Contact _____

Phone (   ) _____ Fax (   ) _____

Access/ATM Card No. _____ Affiliated ATM Card Systems _____

Location of Checks/Book _____

Authorized Signature(s) _____

Financial Institution

Type of Account _____ Account No. _____

Name(s) on Account _____

Address _____

E-Mail Address _____ WW Web Address _____

Contact _____

Phone (   ) _____ Fax (   ) _____

Access/ATM Card No. _____ Affiliated ATM Card Systems _____

Location of Checks/Book _____

Authorized Signature(s) _____

Financial Institution

Type of Account _____ Account No. _____

Name(s) on Account _____

Address _____

E-Mail Address _____ WW Web Address _____

Contact _____

Phone (   ) _____ Fax (   ) _____

Access/ATM Card No. _____ Affiliated ATM Card Systems _____

Location of Checks/Book _____

Authorized Signature(s) _____

Three-hole punch and store any relevant information after this form.

5.2   **Business Accounts**

Complete only those sections or forms that pertain to you.

Date Last Revised
_____

Business Name	Business Type

Address
_____

E-Mail Address	WW Web Address

Phone ( )	Fax ( )

Mobile Phone ( )	Pager/Beeper ( )

Business Accounts Held

For definitions, refer to the glossary.

Financial Institution	Contact

Type of Account	Account No.

Address

E-Mail Address	WW Web Address

Phone ( )	Fax ( )

Access cards may include ATM, credit or debit cards. Indicate the card type and number. Do not indicate the PIN number.

Access/ATM Card No.	Affiliated ATM Card System

Authorized Signature(s)

Location of Checks/Books

Financial Institution	Contact

Type of Account	Account No.

Address

E-Mail Address	WW Web Address

Phone ( )	Fax ( )

Access/ATM Card No.	Affiliated ATM Card System

For additional Business Owned information, refer to Form 8.6.

Authorized Signature(s)

Location of Checks/Books

Financial Institution	Contact

Type of Account	Account No.

Address

E-Mail Address	WW Web Address

Phone ( )	Fax ( )

Access/ATM Card No.	Affiliated ATM Card System

Authorized Signature(s)

Location of Checks/Books

Three-hole punch and store any relevant information after this form.

Business Accounts

Continued

Date Last Revised

Business Name	Business Type
Address	
E-Mail Address	WW Web Address
Phone ( )	Fax ( )
Mobile Phone ( )	Pager/Beeper ( )

Business Accounts Held

For definitions, refer to the glossary.

Financial Institution	Contact
Type of Account	Account No.
Address	
E-Mail Address	WW Web Address
Phone ( )	Fax ( )
Access/ATM Card No.	Affiliated ATM Card System
Authorized Signature(s)	
Location of Checks/Books	

Financial Institution	Contact
Type of Account	Account No.
Address	
E-Mail Address	WW Web Address
Phone ( )	Fax ( )
Access/ATM Card No.	Affiliated ATM Card System
Authorized Signature(s)	
Location of Checks/Books	

Financial Institution	Contact
Type of Account	Account No.
Address	
E-Mail Address	WW Web Address
Phone ( )	Fax ( )
Access/ATM Card No.	Affiliated ATM Card System
Authorized Signature(s)	
Location of Checks/Books	

Three-hole punch and store any relevant information after this form.

5.3 Certificates of Deposit

Complete only those sections or forms that pertain to you.

Date Last Revised

CDs Owned

Financial Institution	Contact
Type of Account	Account No.
Name(s) on Account	
Address	
E-Mail Address	WW Web Address
Phone ( )	Fax ( )
Principal $	Interest Rate %
Date Purchased	Maturity Date
Location of Certificate	
Maturity Instructions	
Financial Institution	Contact
Type of Account	Account No.
Name(s) on Account	
Address	
E-Mail Address	WW Web Address
Phone ( )	Fax ( )
Principal $	Interest Rate %
Date Purchased	Maturity Date
Location of Certificate	
Maturity Instructions	
Financial Institution	Contact
Type of Account	Account No.
Name(s) on Account	
Address	
E-Mail Address	WW Web Address
Phone ( )	Fax ( )
Principal $	Interest Rate %
Date Purchased	Maturity Date
Location of Certificate	
Maturity Instructions	

Three-hole punch and store any relevant information after this form.

Financial Institution   Contact

Type of Account   Account No.

Name(s) on Account

Address

E-Mail Address   WW Web Address

Phone (   )   Fax (   )

Principal $ Interest Rate %

Date Purchased   Maturity Date

Location of Certificate

Maturity Instructions

Financial Institution   Contact

Type of Account   Account No.

Name(s) on Account

Address

E-Mail Address   WW Web Address

Phone (   )   Fax (   )

Principal $ Interest Rate %

Date Purchased   Maturity Date

Location of Certificate

Maturity Instructions

Financial Institution   Contact

Type of Account   Account No.

Name(s) on Account

Address

E-Mail Address   WW Web Address

Phone (   )   Fax (   )

Principal $ Interest Rate %

Date Purchased   Maturity Date

Location of Certificate

Maturity Instructions

Three-hole punch and store any relevant information after this form.

5.4 Loans and Mortgages Owed

Include mortgages, vehicle loans, lines of credit, and all major loans on which you make payments. Also include any other obligations such as promissory notes, educational loans, charge accounts, alimony and child support. Do not include retail or revolving obligations.

Date Last Revised

Owed To

Financial Institution	Contact
Type of Loan	Loan No.
Company Address	
E-Mail Address	WW Web Address
Phone ( )	Fax ( )
Name(s) on Title/Loan	How Held
Interest Rate %	Collateral
Monthly Payment $	Due Date
Final Payment $	Due Date
Date of Notes	Location of Loan Papers

Financial Institution	Contact
Type of Loan	Loan No.
Company Address	
E-Mail Address	WW Web Address
Phone ( )	Fax ( )
Name(s) on Title/Loan	How Held
Interest Rate %	Collateral
Monthly Payment $	Due Date
Final Payment $	Due Date
Date of Notes	Location of Loan Papers

Financial Institution	Contact
Type of Loan	Loan No.
Company Address	
E-Mail Address	WW Web Address
Phone ( )	Fax ( )
Name(s) on Title/Loan	How Held
Interest Rate %	Collateral
Monthly Payment $	Due Date
Final Payment $	Due Date
Date of Notes	Location of Loan Papers

Three-hole punch and store payment schedules, loan agreements and related information behind this form.

Loans and Mortgages Owed

Continued

Financial Institution	Contact
Type of Loan	Loan No.
Company Address	
E-Mail Address	WW Web Address
Phone ( )	Fax ( )
Name(s) on Title/Loan	How Held
Interest Rate %	Collateral
Monthly Payment $	Due Date
Final Payment $	Due Date
Date of Notes	Location of Loan Papers
Financial Institution	Contact
Type of Loan	Loan No.
Company Address	
E-Mail Address	WW Web Address
Phone ( )	Fax ( )
Name(s) on Title/Loan	How Held
Interest Rate %	Collateral
Monthly Payment $	Due Date
Final Payment $	Due Date
Date of Notes	Location of Loan Papers
Financial Institution	Contact
Type of Loan	Loan No.
Company Address	
E-Mail Address	WW Web Address
Phone ( )	Fax ( )
Name(s) on Title/Loan	How Held
Interest Rate %	Collateral
Monthly Payment $	Due Date
Final Payment $	Due Date
Date of Notes	Location of Loan Papers

Three-hole punch and store payment schedules, loan agreements and related information behind this form.

5.5 Loans and Mortgages Owned

Include mortgages and personal loans owed to you. Complete only those sections or forms that pertain to you.

Date Last Revised

Borrower

Type of Loan

Company Address

E-Mail Address   WW Web Address

Phone (   )   Fax (   )

Date of Note   Loan No.

Interest Rate %   Secured/Unsecured

Secured by

Monthly Payment $ Due Date

Final Payment $ Due Date

Location of Loan Papers

Terms of Loan

Three-hole punch and store payment schedules, loan agreements and related information after this form.

Loans and Mortgages Owned

Continued

Borrower

Type of Loan

Company Address

E-Mail Address   WW Web Address

Phone (   )   Fax (   )

Date of Note   Loan No.

Interest Rate %   Secured/Unsecured

Secured by

Monthly Payment $ Due Date

Final Payment $ Due Date

Location of Loan Papers

Terms of Loan

Three-hole punch and
store payment schedules,
loan agreements and
related information after
this form.

6 Personal Securities

Remember to use a pencil on all forms.

PURPOSE

The term *securities* includes investment assets that you can publicly trade, such as stocks, bonds, mutual fund shares, futures contracts, warrants and options.

This section provides forms and worksheets to help you track your various securities from purchase to sale, to document exactly what securities you own and from which company they were purchased.

These forms and worksheets serve two purposes:

- Provide you with instant access to information relating to securities you own and organize them in one place, just in case.
- Provide optional detailed worksheets to which you can refer at income tax time.

Each form contains helpful hints, information and cross-referencing relating to each security.

HOW TO USE THESE FORMS

Fill out the forms, worksheets or lines that apply to you. If you have only one account or if you don't have any, that's fine. Keep the forms for future use as you begin to purchase securities.

As you fill in the information, be sure to document the sale price, amount received, profit/loss and the number of shares sold when you sell that security. Refer to that sale at year-end for income tax reporting.

As you receive your monthly statements, remove outdated statements and save them in a file, three-hole punch the current statement and insert it behind the relating form (if you have chosen to use the loose-leaf notebook format). If you write directly in this kit, indicate on each form where the statements can be located.

Even though you do receive regular statements, it is helpful to document all information from purchase to sale of each security for instant access to that information.

WHEN TO UPDATE

You can update these forms whenever you wish—either as you receive the monthly statements, from current price per share listings in the newspaper or by phoning the company "hot line" for the latest quote.

WHEN TO TOSS

These forms are to be kept and used for a lifetime. Revise information as needed.

OTHER FORMS TO KEEP

If you have documents or information not listed on the form, three-hole punch and insert them in this section.

6.1

Stocks Owned

If your certificates are in your possession, list below the individual stocks you own. If your stock certificates are on deposit at a brokerage, complete the reverse of this form and place a photocopy of your current statement after this form.

Date Last Revised

Name of Stock	Symbol	Exchange	Date Purchased	Certificate No.

For specific tracking of stocks, complete Form 6.2.

Helpful Hint
A *stock split* changes the number of shares but does not change total capital value.

Three-hole punch and store current financial institution's statements after this form. Store all previous statements in an accessible file.

Location of Certificates _____

Stocks Owned

Continued

Complete one entry for each investment brokerage where you have purchased stocks and have a stock certificate on deposit. Also, begin a separate entry for each type of account, for example, an IRA, Keogh or custodial account.

Date Last Revised

Stocks

Investment Brokerage	Account No.
Broker	Type of Account
Address	
Phone ( )	Fax ( )
Mobile Phone ( )	Pager/Beeper ( )
E-Mail Address	WW Web Address
Location of Previous Statements	
Location of Certificates	

Investment Brokerage	Account No.
Broker	Type of Account
Address	
Phone ( )	Fax ( )
Mobile Phone ( )	Pager/Beeper ( )
E-Mail Address	WW Web Address
Location of Previous Statements	
Location of Certificates	

Investment Brokerage	Account No.
Broker	Type of Account
Address	
Phone ( )	Fax ( )
Mobile Phone ( )	Pager/Beeper ( )
E-Mail Address	WW Web Address
Location of Previous Statements	
Location of Certificates	

Three-hole punch and store current financial institution's statements after this form. Store all previous statements in an accessible file.

6.2　Stock Record

This worksheet allows you to easily track all the stocks you buy and sell. It's especially helpful when reporting yearly stock sales for income tax returns.

Date Last Revised _____

Name of Stock	Date Purchased	Original No. of Shares	Original Price Per Share	Total Cost
			$	$

Helpful Hint
Keep records at least seven years after sale of stock.

A *stock split* is a change in the number of shares, but does not change their total capital value.

6.2

Stock Record

Continued

A *common stock* is a share or a portion of ownership in a company.

Stock Split Date	Current No. of Shares	Current Price Per Share	Current Value	Date Sold	No. of Shares Sold	Amount Received	Profit(Loss)
		$	$			$	$

6.3 Stock Price Per Share

This form enables you to chart the price per share of your currently owned individual stocks. It can help you evaluate whether to buy, hold or sell additional shares. Monthly, or periodically, enter the current *price per share* of the individual stock in the appropriate space and then review the progress of each stock. When you sell a stock, erase the information pertaining to that stock so you can enter a newly purchased stock.

	Date	Date	Date	Date	Date	Date	Date	Date	Date
	___	___	___	___	___	___	___	___	___

Name of Stock	Price	Price	Price	Price	Price	Price	Price	Price	Price
	$	$	$	$	$	$	$	$	$

Three-hole punch and store any relevant information after this form.

6.3

Stock Price Per Share
Continued

	Date	Date	Date	Date	Date	Date	Date	Date	Date
Name of Stock	Price	Price	Price	Price	Price	Price	Price	Price	Price
	$	$	$	$	$	$	$	$	$

Three-hole punch and store any
relevant information after this form.

6.4

Bonds Owned

If you hold registered bonds in your possession, list the individual bonds below. If your bonds are in book entry form on deposit at a financial institution, complete the reverse side of this form. Place a copy of your most current statement after this form.

Date Last Revised

Name of Bond	Type of Bond	Issue Date	Interest	Certificate No.	Maturity Date

For specific tracking of bonds, refer to Form 6.5, "Bond Record."

Bond Types
Treasury bonds, savings bonds, government agency securities, mortgage-backed securities, municipal bonds, corporate bonds, foreign bonds, convertible bonds, zero-coupon bonds, etc.

Location of Certificates _____

Three-hole punch and store relevant information after this form.

Bonds Owned

Continued

List all financial institutions where bonds are held in each separate entry for each type of account, for example, an IRA, Keogh or custodial account.

Date Last Revised

Bonds

For specific tracking of bonds, refer to Form 6.5, "Bond Record."

If you own book entry bonds and there is activity in your account, you will receive a monthly statement. If there is no activity in your account, you will receive a quarterly statement.

Investment Brokerage   Account No.

Broker   Type of Account

Address

E-Mail Address   WW Web Address

Phone (   )   Fax (   )

Mobile Phone (   )   Pager/Beeper (   )

Location of Previous Statements

Investment Brokerage   Account No.

Broker   Type of Account

Address

E-Mail Address   WW Web Address

Phone (   )   Fax (   )

Mobile Phone (   )   Pager/Beeper (   )

Location of Previous Statements

Investment Brokerage   Account No.

Broker   Type of Account

Address

E-Mail Address   WW Web Address

Phone (   )   Fax (   )

Mobile Phone (   )   Pager/Beeper (   )

Location of Previous Statements

Investment Brokerage   Account No.

Broker   Type of Account

Address

E-Mail Address   WW Web Address

Phone (   )   Fax (   )

Mobile Phone (   )   Pager/Beeper (   )

Location of Previous Statements

Three-hole punch and store relevant information after this form.

6.5

Bond Record

This worksheet is optional. When properly completed in pencil, a running record of all bonds owned and sold can be tracked for easy reference. It's especially helpful when reporting for income tax returns.

Date Last Revised _____

Name of Bond	Bond No. or Book Entry No.	Type of Bond	Price of Bond
			$

Helpful Hint
Keep records at least seven years after sale of bond.

Date of Issue	Sale/Maturity Date	Current Interest Yield	Tax Status*	Conversion Callable Features	Net Sales Price	Net Gain/Loss
					$	$

When you invest in a bond, you are loaning the issuer of that bond your money in return for a fixed rate of interest for a specific amount of time, usually receiving interest every six months. When the bond matures, you receive your original principal.

To chart the current interest yield, erase the old yield and enter the current interest yield in the column above when current statement is received.

*Tax Status Key
T = Taxable
E1 = Exempt State
E2 = Exempt Federal
E3 = Exempt Both

6.6

Mutual Funds Held

Mutual fund company investments generally operate in one of two ways: directly, or through an investment brokerage company or bank. As appropriate, complete this information for your funds held. Complete one fund per each side of form.

For definitions of types of funds and to track specific funds, refer to Form 6.7, **"Mutual Funds at a Glance."**

A *mutual fund* is a large portfolio of selected securities managed by a professional manager or management team.

Helpful Hint
It is essential to keep your end of the year mutual fund statements seven years after selling the fund.

Date Last Revised

Name of Fund	Fund Account No.
Type of Fund	
Fund Fees*	
Transfer/Trading Phone ( )	
Customer Service Phone ( )	
Quotations Phone ( )	Fax ( )
Title on Account	
Date Opened	Original Investment $
Beneficiary	
Secondary Beneficiary	
Was a Certificate Issued?	Certificate Location
Investment Brokerage	Account No.
Address	
E-Mail Address	WW Web Address
Contact	
Phone ( )	Fax ( )
Mobile Phone ( )	Pager/Beeper ( )

Notes

Three-hole punch and store the current and the year-end statement for each fund held after this form.

*Fund Fees Include
- Annual Management
- 12 b-1
- Exit or Redemption

Mutual Funds Held

Continued

Date Last Revised

Name of Fund   Fund Account No.

Type of Fund

Fund Fees

Transfer/Trading Phone (   )

The dollar value of one share of a fund's stock is its net asset value (NAV).

Customer Service Phone (   )

Quotations Phone (   )   Fax (   )

Title on Account

Date Opened   Original Investment $

Beneficiary

Secondary Beneficiary

Was a Certificate Issued?   Certificate Location

Investment Brokerage   Account No.

Address

E-Mail Address   WW Web Address

Contact

Phone (   )   Fax (   )

Mobile Phone (   )   Pager/Beeper (   )

Notes

Three-hole punch and store the year-end and the most recent statement for each fund held after this form.

6.7   Mutual Funds at a Glance

A *mutual fund* is a large portfolio of selected securities often including between 30 and 300 different stocks, bonds and other investments. It is managed by a professional manager or management team.

TYPES OF MUTUAL FUNDS

Aggressive Growth Funds

These funds invest in new companies.

Balanced Funds

These funds invest in combination of bonds, preferred and common stock.

Bond Funds

These funds invest in government, corporate or tax-exempt bonds with varying maturities:

Short term	few years
Intermediate	7–10 years
Long-term	20 years +

Closed-End Funds

A fixed number of shares are available for these funds. The fund raises money at one time. Shares often trade at a discount from selling price.

Global Funds

These funds invest in foreign and U.S. securities.

Growth Funds

These funds invest in established companies whose earnings expect to increase.

Growth and Income Funds

These funds invest in companies with growth potential and pay good dividends.

Income Funds

These funds invest in income producing securities.

International Stock/Bond Funds

These funds invest internationally.

Load Funds

Owner pays commission on purchase of these funds, and often on reinvested dividends.

No-Load Funds

No commission is paid for purchase of these funds. Fees might be charged for sales and marketing cost, however.

Open-End Funds

With these funds, you can continue to invest in shares.

Option Income Funds

These funds invest in dividend-paying common stock on which call options are traded.

Small Company Growth Funds

These funds specialize in small companies.

6.7 Mutual Fund Record

This worksheet allows you to keep a running record of all funds owned and sold. It's especially helpful when reporting yearly fund sales for income tax returns.

Date Last Revised _____

Fund Name	Fund Type	Date Purchased	Original No. of Shares	Original Price Per Share	Total Cost	Date Reinvested Shares	Current No. of Shares

Helpful Hint
Keep records at least seven years after sale of fund.

6.7

Mutual Fund Record

Continued

Distributions of mutual fund gains can be through regular checks, deposits to another account, reinvestments in the same fund or a combination. Taxable earnings must be reported to IRS even if reinvested.

Current Price Per Share	Current Value	Dividend Income	Date Sold	No. of Shares Sold	Amount Received	Profit (Loss)	Annual Mgmt. Fee*

In a family of funds, a mutual fund company can offer several different funds; you can switch shares among them.

*Management Fees Include
- Annual Management
- 12b-1
- Exit or redemption

6.8 Limited Partnerships

Complete only those sections or forms that pertain to you. Fill out one form per limited partnership.

Date Last Revised _____

Name of Investment _____ Investment Type _____

Investment Address _____

A *limited partnership* is a money-raising or investment device that allows partnership businesses to raise money without taking in new owners. This is accomplished by selling partnership shares in the business.

General Partner _____ Tax ID No. _____

Address _____

E-Mail Address _____ WW Web Address _____

Phone (   ) _____ Fax (   ) _____

Mobile Phone (   ) _____ Pager/Beeper (   ) _____

Location of Records _____

For additional information, refer to K1 of your federal and state income tax returns.

Original Amount Invested	**Date Invested**	**Total Invested to Date**
$		$

Types of limited partnerships include investments in real estate, oil, gas and restaurants, etc.

Income Received	**Date Received**	**Total Income to Date**
$		$

Three-hole punch and store any relevant information behind this form.

Date Partnership Ended _____

Total Profit/Loss $ _____

Limited Partnerships

Continued

Date Last Revised

Name of Investment

Investment Address

General Partner	Tax ID No. of General Partner
Address	
E-Mail Address	WW Web Address
Phone ( )	Fax ( )
Mobile Phone ( )	Pager/Beeper ( )
Location of Records	

Original Amount Invested	Date Invested	Total Invested to Date
$		$
$		$
$		$
$		$
$		$
$		$
$		$

For additional information, refer to K1 of income tax return.

Income Received	Date Received	Total Income to Date
$		$
$		$
$		$
$		$
$		$
$		$
$		$

Three-hole punch and store any relevant information behind this form.

Date Partnership Ended

Total Profit/Loss $

6.9

Annuities

Complete only those sections or forms that pertain to you.

Annuities are issued by life insurance companies and pay income while you are alive, usually after you retire.

Two kinds of annuities are available: immediate and deferred.

An *immediate annuity* is purchased with a single payment and payout can begin immediately or within the first year.

With a *deferred annuity*, earnings grow tax-free during an accumulation period. Payout can begin at age 59½.

Three-hole punch and store any relevant information behind this form.

Date Last Revised

Name of Annuitant | Annuity Type

Policy/Contract No.

Issue Date | Issue Age

Maturity Date | Maturity Age

Annuity Owner

Address

E-Mail Address | WW Web Address

Phone ( ) | Fax ( )

Policy Company Name

Address

Phone ( ) | Fax ( )

Insurance Agent's Company Name | Agent's Name

Address

E-Mail Address | WW Web Address

Phone ( ) | Fax ( )

Mobile Phone ( ) | Pager/Beeper ( )

Is the Premium Periodic or Lump Sum? | Amount $

Is the Premium Fixed, Flexible or Single?

Is the Premium Frequency Monthly, Quarterly, Semi-Annually or Annually?

Are Income Provisions Immediate or Deferred?

Surrender Charges

Beneficiary

Second Beneficiary

Annuities

Continued

Date Last Revised
_____

Name of Annuitant _____ Annuity Type _____

Policy/Contract No. _____

Issue Date _____ Issue Age _____

Maturity Date _____ Maturity Age _____

Annuity Owner _____

Address _____

E-Mail Address _____ WW Web Address _____

Phone (   ) _____ Fax (   ) _____

Policy Company Name _____

Address _____

Phone (   ) _____ Fax (   ) _____

Insurance Agent's Company Name _____ Agent's Name _____

Address _____

E-Mail Address _____ WW Web Address _____

Phone (   ) _____ Fax (   ) _____

Mobile Phone (   ) _____ Pager/Beeper (   ) _____

Is the Premium Periodic or Lump Sum? _____ Amount $ _____

Is the Premium Fixed, Flexible or Single? _____

Is the Premium Frequency Monthly, Quarterly, Semi-Annually or Annually? _____

Are Income Provisions Immediate or Deferred? _____

Surrender Charges _____

Beneficiary _____

Second Beneficiary _____

Three-hole punch and
store any relevant
information behind this
form.

7 Other Financial Interests

Remember to use a pencil on all forms.

PURPOSE

This section includes Custodial Accounts, Trust Accounts and Retirement Accounts.

To retire you should plan on a yearly retirement income to equal 80% to 100% of your yearly salary income. During your earning years, you should be or should have invested in various retirement accounts in order to attain those needs: IRAs, 401(k)s, 403(b)s, profit-sharing or SARs, etc.

This section provides Retirement Account forms on which to document these investments. Form 7.3, **"Trust Accounts,"** is designed to document any trust accounts set up by you or for which you are the beneficiary. Form 7.1, **"Custodial Accounts,"** lists any assets for which you or your spouse act as guardian over a minor child, elderly parents or other dependents.

**HOW TO USE
THESE FORMS**

Fill out only those forms or the lines that apply to you. If you do not need this section now, simply go on to the next section.

WHEN TO UPDATE

Be sure to update all information and changes as they occur. As you acquire new accounts, be sure to enter them in this section.

WHEN TO TOSS

Keep these forms for your lifetime. When information changes, erase the old and enter the new in pencil.

**OTHER FORMS
TO KEEP**

If you have documents or information not listed on the forms, three-hole punch and insert them in this section.

7.1

Custodial Accounts

List all assets held for dependent or minor below. Complete only those sections or forms that pertain to you.

Date Last Revised _____

Minor or Dependent's Name	Guardian's Name
Social Security No.	Date of Birth

Address _____

Phone (   ) _____

Fax (   ) _____

A *custodial account* is an account that is established for a guardian to oversee the assets of a minor.

Laws may vary from state to state. Check your state laws regarding the Uniform Gifts to Minors Act.

Assets	Value
1	$
2	
3	
4	
5	
6	
7	
8	
9	
10	
11	
12	
13	
14	
15	
16	
17	
18	
19	
20	

For additional asset listings, continue on back of this form.

Three-hole punch and store any relevant information after this form.

Custodial Accounts

Continued

Assets	Value
21	$
22	
23	
24	
25	
26	
27	
28	
29	
30	
31	
32	
33	
34	
35	
36	
37	
38	
39	
40	
41	
42	
43	
44	
45	

Total Assets $

Three-hole punch and store any relevant information after this form.

7.1 Custodial Accounts

List all assets held for dependent or minor below. Complete only those sections or forms that pertain to you.

Date Last Revised

Minor or Dependent's Name	Guardian's Name
Social Security No.	Date of Birth
Address	
Phone ( )	
Fax ( )	

Assets	**Value**
1	$
2	
3	
4	
5	
6	
7	
8	
9	
10	
11	
12	
13	
14	
15	
16	
17	
18	
19	
20	

A *custodial account* is an account that is established for a guardian to oversee the assets of a minor.

Laws may vary from state to state. Check your state laws regarding the Uniform Gifts to Minors Act.

For additional asset listings, continue on back of this form.

Three-hole punch and store any relevant information after this form.

Continued

Assets	Value
21	$
22	
23	
24	
25	
26	
27	
28	
29	
30	
31	
32	
33	
34	
35	
36	
37	
38	
39	
40	
41	
42	
43	
44	
45	

Total Assets $

Three-hole punch and store any relevant information after this form.

7.2

Retirement Accounts

Complete one form per family member. Be sure to include each of the different retirement funds you have. For example: IRAs, 401(k)s, 403(b)s, company stock ownership, profit-sharing, SARs, SAR/SEPTs and pensions.

Date Last Revised

Family Member's Name

Type of Retirement Account

Company Holding Fund

Address

E-Mail Address	WW Web Address
Phone ( )	Fax ( )
Account Number	Date of Maturity

Beneficiary

Percent of Gross Income Applied %	Predicted Balance $

Location of Further Information

Age or Year Fund Is Available	Early Withdrawal Penalty Charge $

Type of Retirement Account

Company Holding Fund

Address

E-Mail Address	WW Web Address
Phone ( )	Fax ( )
Account Number	Date of Maturity

Beneficiary

Percent of Gross Income Applied %	Predicted Balance $

Location of Further Information

Age or Year Fund Is Available	Early Withdrawal Penalty Charge $

Type of Retirement Account

Company Holding Fund

Address

E-Mail Address	WW Web Address
Phone ( )	Fax ( )
Account Number	Date of Maturity

Beneficiary

Percent of Gross Income Applied %	Predicted Balance $

Location of Further Information

Age or Year Fund Is Available	Early Withdrawal Penalty Charge $

Helpful Hints
Consider extending your working years to allow more time for your investments, Social Security benefits, and pension benefits to grow.

Obtain your current Social Security personal earning and benefit estimate by completing a Request for Earnings and Benefits Statement, Form SSA-7004, from your local Social Security office. Do this at least every five years.

Three-hole punch and store current statements and any other relevant information after this form.

Retirement Accounts

Continued

Type of Retirement Account

Company Holding Fund

Address

E-Mail Address	WW Web Address
Phone ( )	Fax ( )
Account Number	Date of Maturity

Beneficiary

Percent of Gross Income Applied %	Predicted Balance $

Location of Further Information

Age or Year Fund Is Available	Early Withdrawal Penalty Charge $

Type of Retirement Account

Company Holding Fund

Address

E-Mail Address	WW Web Address
Phone ( )	Fax ( )
Account Number	Date of Maturity

Beneficiary

Percent of Gross Income Applied %	Predicted Balance $

Location of Further Information

Age or Year Fund Is Available	Early Withdrawal Penalty Charge $

Type of Retirement Account

Company Holding Fund

Address

E-Mail Address	WW Web Address
Phone ( )	Fax ( )
Account Number	Date of Maturity

Beneficiary

Percent of Gross Income Applied %	Predicted Balance $

Location of Further Information

Age or Year Fund Is Available	Early Withdrawal Penalty Charge $

Three-hole punch and store current statements and any other relevant information after this form.

7.2

Retirement Accounts

Complete one form per family member. Be sure to include each of the different retirement funds you have. For example: IRAs, 401(k)s, 403(b)s, company stock ownership, profit-sharing, SARs, SAR/SEPTs and pensions.

Date Last Revised

Family Member's Name

Type of Retirement Account

Company Holding Fund

Address

E-Mail Address | WW Web Address

Phone ( ) | Fax ( )

Account Number | Date of Maturity

Beneficiary

Percent of Gross Income Applied % | Predicted Balance $

Location of Further Information

Age or Year Fund Is Available | Early Withdrawal Penalty Charge $

Type of Retirement Account

Company Holding Fund

Address

E-Mail Address | WW Web Address

Phone ( ) | Fax ( )

Account Number | Date of Maturity

Beneficiary

Percent of Gross Income Applied % | Predicted Balance $

Location of Further Information

Age or Year Fund Is Available | Early Withdrawal Penalty Charge $

Type of Retirement Account

Company Holding Fund

Address

E-Mail Address | WW Web Address

Phone ( ) | Fax ( )

Account Number | Date of Maturity

Beneficiary

Percent of Gross Income Applied % | Predicted Balance $

Location of Further Information

Age or Year Fund Is Available | Early Withdrawal Penalty Charge $

Helpful Hints
Consider extending your working years to allow more time for your investments, Social Security benefits, and pension benefits to grow.

Obtain your current Social Security personal earning and benefit estimate by completing a Request for Earnings and Benefits Statement, Form SSA-7004, from your local Social Security office. Do this at least every five years.

Three-hole punch and store current statements and any other relevant information after this form.

Type of Retirement Account

Company Holding Fund

Address

E-Mail Address | WW Web Address

Phone (   ) | Fax (   )

Account Number | Date of Maturity

Beneficiary

Percent of Gross Income Applied % | Predicted Balance $

Location of Further Information

Age or Year Fund Is Available | Early Withdrawal Penalty Charge $

Type of Retirement Account

Company Holding Fund

Address

E-Mail Address | WW Web Address

Phone (   ) | Fax (   )

Account Number | Date of Maturity

Beneficiary

Percent of Gross Income Applied % | Predicted Balance $

Location of Further Information

Age or Year Fund Is Available | Early Withdrawal Penalty Charge $

Type of Retirement Account

Company Holding Fund

Address

E-Mail Address | WW Web Address

Phone (   ) | Fax (   )

Account Number | Date of Maturity

Beneficiary

Percent of Gross Income Applied % | Predicted Balance $

Location of Further Information

Age or Year Fund Is Available | Early Withdrawal Penalty Charge $

Three-hole punch and store current statements and any other relevant information after this form.

7.3

Trust Accounts

Complete this form for a trust that you have established or for a trust for which you are a beneficiary.

Date Last Revised
_____

Name of Trust _____ Type of Trust _____

Established by _____ Date Established _____

Name of Trustee _____

Address _____

Phone (   ) _____ Fax (   ) _____

Name of Attorney _____

Name of Firm _____

Address _____

Purpose of Trust _____

Income Provisions _____

Principle Provisions _____

Income Beneficiary _____

Remainderman Beneficiary _____

Date of Amendment 1 _____

Purpose of Amendment 1 _____

_____

_____

Date of Amendment 2 _____

Purpose of Amendment 2 _____

_____

_____

Location of Original Trust Agreements _____

_____

Helpful Hints

- A *trust* is a legal entity that holds title to your assets. You are the trustee of the trust, so you maintain full control over your assets. The most important reason for having a trust is to avoid the cost and agony of probate.

- *Remainderman* is one who has an interest in an estate and receives the benefit of that estate upon its termination.

Three-hole punch and store a copy of the trust agreement and the most current statement after this form.

Name of Trust

Type of Trust

Established by

Date Established

Name of Trustee

Address

Phone (   )

Fax (   )

Name of Attorney

Name of Firm

Address

Purpose of Trust

Income Provisions

Principle Provisions

Income Beneficiary

Remainderman Beneficiary

Date of Amendment 1

Purpose of Amendment 1

Date of Amendment 2

Purpose of Amendment 2

Location of Original Trust Agreements

Three-hole punch and store a copy of the trust agreement and the most current statement after this form.

8 Personal Property

Remember to use a pencil on all forms.

PURPOSE

It is very important to document the existence, value and location of all your personal property. This includes all tangible and hard assets, especially those of value (refer to individual forms for definitions). In case of loss of your highly valued items, your insurance company may ask for purchase and value verification—requiring receipts and written appraisals. Without proof of value, you risk receiving a devalued reimbursement of your loss.

In addition to documenting and holding appraisals and receipts, you might consider videotaping all personal property owned. This includes opening cupboards, drawers and garage and videotaping all their contents. Not only will this provide proof of ownership, it will jog your memory in case a major disaster occurs.

This section includes forms on which to list all personal property owned and to document the location of all safe-deposit boxes, home safes or locked boxes where appraisals, receipts or valued items are stored. Form 8.5, **"Vehicles Owned,"** is designed to document complete ownership and sales of all vehicles. A registration fee chart provides an at-a-glance summary of fees paid on each vehicle in prior years. If you own your own business, Form 8.6, **"Businesses Owned,"** documents all details about that business. Once filled out, in case of need, anyone can refer to that form and instantly be informed of business ownership and financial details.

HOW TO USE THESE FORMS

Fill out only those forms or the lines that apply to you. If you've chosen the loose-leaf binder format, you can three-hole punch the purchased white 8¾″ × 11¾″ envelope and insert it behind Form 8.4, **"Appraisals and Sales Receipts,"** to hold all photocopies of appraisals and sales receipts. This helps to provide instant access to proof of ownership and personal property value, if necessary.

If you are using this kit, place the appraisals and sales receipts in the envelope, store it in a safe location and document the envelope's location directly on Form 8.4.

WHEN TO UPDATE

Update all information and changes as they occur. Refer to instructions on each form. When you sell a vehicle, it is a good idea to keep the records for seven years after selling the vehicle as proof of sale and of buyer. Before erasing information of the sold vehicle, photocopy the form, three-hole punch it and insert it in your kit.

WHEN TO TOSS

Keep these forms for your lifetime. When information changes, erase the old and enter the new in pencil.

OTHER FORMS TO KEEP

If you have documents or information not listed on the forms, three-hole punch and insert them in this section.

8.1

Storage of Valuables

Figure out a fail-safe method for recording safe-deposit box and home-safe combinations; key, home-safe, safe-deposit box locations; and storage rental unit combinations and locations. Tell a trusted family member, executor, attorney, friend or as many as those listed with whom you feel comfortable.

Date Last Revised

Safe Deposit Box or Vault Number

Names with Right of Entry

Financial Institution

Address

Phone (   )   Fax (   )

Location of Inventory List

Home Safe Location

Location of Inventory List

Access Instructions in Case of Emergency

Fire-Proof Locked Box

Location

Location of Inventory List

Access Instructions in Case of Emergency

Other

Location

Location of Inventory List

Contents

Access Instructions in Case of Emergency

Helpful Hints

• An inexpensive way to organize infrequently used keys is to color-code or number-code them. Record the colors or numbers and store this information in a safe and separate location.

• Keep your spare keys organized in a locked key cabinet purchased from your hardware store.

• One of the biggest problems with combinations is that you must remember them even if you use them infrequently. Depending upon your personal circumstances, consider writing down combinations and giving a copy of this information to a trusted friend, associate, executor or attorney.

Three-hole punch and store any relevant information after this form.

Storage of Valuables

Continued

Other

Location

Location of Inventory List

Contents

_____

_____

_____

Access Instructions in Case of Emergency

_____

Other

Location

Location of Inventory List

Contents

_____

_____

_____

Access Instructions in Case of Emergency

_____

Other

Location

Location of Inventory List

Contents

_____

_____

_____

Access Instructions in Case of Emergency

_____

If you rent an outside storage unit for furniture or other personal items, be sure to list the items stored, location and combination to the unit on this form.

Three-hole punch and store any relevant information after this form.

8.2

Tangible Assets Inventory

List personal property and tangible assets, including antiques, artwork, cameras, computers, fine arts, furs, guns, heirlooms, jewelry, musical instruments, silverware and any other valuables or collectibles. Complete only those forms that pertain to you.

Date Last Revised

Item	Location

Description

Where Purchased	Location of Receipt
Date Purchased	Cost $
Date of Last Appraisal	Value $
Location of Last Appraisal	Location of Photos or Videos

Is This Item Covered on Your Personal Property Insurance?　　　Amount $

Item	Location

Description

Where Purchased	Location of Receipt
Date Purchased	Cost $
Date of Last Appraisal	Value $
Location of Last Appraisal	Location of Photos or Videos

Is This Item Covered on Your Personal Property Insurance?　　　Amount $

Item	Location

Description

Where Purchased	Location of Receipt
Date Purchased	Cost $
Date of Last Appraisal	Value $
Location of Last Appraisal	Location of Photos or Videos

Is This Item Covered on Your Personal Property Insurance?　　　Amount $

Item	Location

Description

Where Purchased	Location of Receipt
Date Purchased	Cost $
Date of Last Appraisal	Value $
Location of Last Appraisal	Location of Photos or Videos

Is This Item Covered on Your Personal Property Insurance?　　　Amount $

Helpful Hints
- Take photographs or videos of your possessions, including the insides of drawers, closets and cupboards. Store these pictures away from your residence, such as in a safe deposit box. Give an additional copy of the photo or video record to a family member, a trusted friend, associate or your attorney.

- Writing down the location of valued items will help you avoid misplacing those items and will help establish proof in case of loss.

Store photocopies of original receipts after Form 8.4, "Appraisals and Sales Receipts."

Tangible Assets Inventory

Continued

Date Last Revised

Item	Location
Description	
Where Purchased	Location of Receipt
Date Purchased	Cost $
Date of Last Appraisal	Value $
Location of Last Appraisal	Location of Photos or Videos
Is This Item Covered on Your Personal Property Insurance?	Amount $
Item	Location
Description	
Where Purchased	Location of Receipt
Date Purchased	Cost $
Date of Last Appraisal	Value $
Location of Last Appraisal	Location of Photos or Videos
Is This Item Covered on Your Personal Property Insurance?	Amount $
Item	Location
Description	
Where Purchased	Location of Receipt
Date Purchased	Cost $
Date of Last Appraisal	Value $
Location of Last Appraisal	Location of Photos or Videos
Is This Item Covered on Your Personal Property Insurance?	Amount $
Item	Location
Description	
Where Purchased	Location of Receipt
Date Purchased	Cost $
Date of Last Appraisal	Value $
Location of Last Appraisal	Location of Photos or Videos
Is This Item Covered on Your Personal Property Insurance?	Amount $

Store photocopies of
original receipts after
Form 8.4.

8.3

Hard Assets Inventory

List all gems, gold, silver, bullion, other precious metals, etc. Also list stamps, coins, medallions and any other hard assets you own. Only complete those pages or forms that pertain to you.

Date Last Revised

Item

Description

Where Purchased | Location of Receipt

Date Purchased | Cost $

Date of Last Appraisal | Value $

Location of Last Appraisal

Date Sold | Amount Received $

Is This Item Covered on Your Personal Property Insurance? | Amount $

Storage Location of Asset

Location of Photos or Videos

Item

Description

Where Purchased | Location of Receipt

Date Purchased | Cost $

Date of Last Appraisal | Value $

Location of Last Appraisal

Date Sold | Amount Received $

Is This Item Covered on Your Personal Property Insurance? | Amount $

Storage Location of Asset

Location of Photos or Videos

Item

Description

Where Purchased | Location of Receipt

Date Purchased | Cost $

Date of Last Appraisal | Value $

Location of Last Appraisal

Date Sold | Amount Received $

Is This Item Covered on Your Personal Property Insurance? | Amount $

Storage Location of Asset

Location of Photos or Videos

Store photocopies of original receipts after Form 8.4, "Appraisals and Sales Receipts."

Hard Assets Inventory

Continued

Date Last Revised

Item

Description

Where Purchased	Location of Receipt
Date Purchased	Cost $
Date of Last Appraisal	Value $

Location of Last Appraisal

Date Sold	Amount Received $

Is This Item Covered on Your Personal Property Insurance?   Amount $

Storage Location of Asset

Location of Photos or Videos

Item

Description

Where Purchased	Location of Receipt
Date Purchased	Cost $
Date of Last Appraisal	Value $

Location of Last Appraisal

Date Sold	Amount Received $

Is This Item Covered on Your Personal Property Insurance?   Amount $

Storage Location of Asset

Location of Photos or Videos

Item

Description

Where Purchased	Location of Receipt
Date Purchased	Cost $
Date of Last Appraisal	Value $

Location of Last Appraisal

Date Sold	Amount Received $

Is This Item Covered on Your Personal Property Insurance?   Amount $

Storage Location of Asset

Location of Photos or Videos

Store photocopies of
original receipts after
Form 8.4.

8.4　Appraisals and Sales Receipts

List appraisals and sales receipts of large-ticket items below. Store original sales receipts and appraisals in your safe-deposit box. If you are using the binder format, three-hole punch your purchased 8¾″ × 11¾″ envelope and insert it behind this form. Place photocopies of all receipts and appraisals in it.

Date Last Revised

Item Description	$ Value	Location of Original	Location of Photocopy

Helpful Hint
Save receipts of high-ticket items as proof in case of damage or loss.

For a complete list of inventory, refer to Forms 8.2, "Tangible Assets Inventory," and 8.3, "Hard Assets Inventory."

Vehicles Owned

Complete a separate form for each vehicle you own or lease. Complete only those sections or forms that pertain to you.

Date Last Revised

Vehicle Information

Make/Model

Year | License No.

Vehicle ID No.

Date Purchase/Lease | Purchase/Lease Price $

Financial Information

Purchased/Leased From

Address

E-Mail Address

Contact | Phone (   )

New or Used | Fax (   )

Odometer Reading at Time of Purchase

Amount of Sales Tax Paid $ | Date Paid

License Fee Paid $ | Date Paid

Financed By | Account No.

Address

E-Mail Address

Phone (   ) | Fax (   )

Original Amount Owed $

Monthly Payments $ | Due Date

Location of Ownership Papers

Sold To | Odometer Reading

Address | Date Sold

Phone (   ) | Fax (   )

Sale Price $ | Date Notified DMV of Sale

Location of Ownership Papers | Drivers License No.

Registration Information

Registration Fee Due Date

Helpful Hints

- Photocopy current vehicle registration slip and keep in vehicle glove box. Keep original in a safe-deposit box.

- It is a good idea to keep this form in your records for seven years after selling the vehicle as proof of sale and of buyer.

Registration Fee Chart
This chart is helpful in comparing prior years' registration fees on your vehicle. If you have access to prior years' fees paid, fill in the chart accordingly. For subsequent years, fill in the chart at the time fees are paid.

Year	Amount	Year	Amount
	$		$
	$		$
	$		$
	$		$

Vehicles Owned

Continued

Date Last Revised

Vehicle Information

Make/Model

Year   License No.

Vehicle ID No.

Date Purchase/Lease   Purchase/Lease Price $

Financial Information

Purchased/Leased From

Address

E-Mail Address

Contact   Phone (   )

New or Used   Fax (   )

Odometer Reading at Time of Purchase

Amount of Sales Tax Paid $ Date Paid

License Fee Paid $ Date Paid

Financed By   Account No.

Address

E-Mail Address

Phone (   )   Fax (   )

Original Amount Owed $

Monthly Payments $ Due Date

Location of Ownership Papers

Sold To   Odometer Reading

Address   Date Sold

Phone (   )   Fax (   )

Sale Price $ Date Notified DMV of Sale

Location of Ownership Papers   Drivers License No.

Registration Information

Registration Fee Due Date

Helpful Hints
- Photocopy current vehicle registration slip and keep in vehicle glove box. Keep original in a safe-deposit box.

- It is a good idea to keep this form in your records for seven years after selling the vehicle as proof of sale and of buyer.

Registration Fee Chart
This chart is helpful in comparing prior years' registration fees on your vehicle. If you have access to prior years' fees paid, fill in the chart accordingly. For subsequent years, fill in the chart at the time fees are paid.

Year	Amount	Year	Amount
	$		$
	$		$
	$		$
	$		$

8.6 Businesses Owned

Complete only those sections or forms that pertain to you.

Forms of business ownership include sole ownership, tenants in common, joint tenancy with right of survivorship, tenancy by the entirety, and community property.

See reverse side for corporation definitions, and for names and addresses of each partner involved in this business.

Consult with an attorney and tax professional knowledgeable in corporate and partnership issues before deciding to incorporate and for indepth explanations on incorporating.

Date Last Revised

Business Information

Business Name

Address

E-Mail Address   WW Web Address

Phone (   )   Fax (   )

Mobile Phone (   )   Pager/Beeper (   )

Form of Ownership

Incorporated?   Type of Corporation

Description of Business

Business in the Name(s) of

Percentage of Ownership

Business Value $ Gross Annual Income $

Business License No.   Tax ID No.

Other Business License No.

Property Information

Owned Property   Value $ Monthly Payments $

Final Payment Due Date   Final Payment $

Paid to Whom

Leased Property   Payment $ Length of Lease

Landlord's Name   Date Lease Expires

Address

Phone (   )   Fax (   )

Other

Location of Instructions in Case of Disability or Death

Location of All Agreements if This Kit Is Being Used To Document All Information*

*If using this kit format, indicate above where all partnership, corporate ownership agreements or any other relevant information is being stored.

If using the loose-leaf binder, photocopy, three-hole punch and store partnership or corporate ownership agreements or any other relevant information after this form. See Form 1.2 for locations of original agreements.

Businesses Owned

Continued

Date Last Revised

Partners

Name	Mobile Phone ( )
Address	
E-Mail Address	Phone ( )
Pager/Beeper ( )	Fax ( )
Percentage of Ownership	Original Investment $
Business License Number	Tax ID Number
Other Business License Number	

Name	Mobile Phone ( )
Address	
E-Mail Address	Phone ( )
Pager/Beeper ( )	Fax ( )
Percentage of Ownership	Original Investment $
Business License Number	Tax ID Number
Other Business License Number	

Name	Mobile Phone ( )
Address	
E-Mail Address	Phone ( )
Pager/Beeper ( )	Fax ( )
Percentage of Ownership	Original Investment $
Business License Number	Tax ID Number
Other Business License Number	

Name	Mobile Phone ( )
Address	
E-Mail Address	Phone ( )
Pager/Beeper ( )	Fax ( )
Percentage of Ownership	Original Investment $
Business License Number	Tax ID Number
Other Business License Number	

9   Real Estate

Remember to use a pencil on each form.

PURPOSE

Real estate ownership can range from owning your own home, second home, condo, co-op apartment, apartment building, a real estate partnership or barren land in the desert.

It is one of the few investment areas where deductions are allowed for mortgage interest and property taxes. In addition, rental property can be depreciated to reduce your taxable income.

This section will help you document addresses and financial details of all your real estate property. The forms include helpful hints and space in which to list property improvement dates and financial details for income tax deductions. By filling in all details, you are providing instant access to information you need for loan applications as well as for the one in charge, just in case.

HOW TO USE THESE FORMS

Fill out only those forms that apply to you. If you do not own any real estate at this time, continue to the next section.

WHEN TO UPDATE

Update all information and changes as they occur. Refer to instructions and helpful hints on each form. When you sell a property, it is a good idea to keep the records for at least seven years after selling the property for tax purposes, proof of sale and to whom it was sold. Before erasing information on sold property, photocopy the form, three-hole punch it and insert it in your kit.

WHEN TO TOSS

Keep these forms for your lifetime. When information changes, erase the old and enter the new in pencil.

OTHER FORMS TO KEEP

If you have documents or information not listed on the forms, three-hole punch and insert them in this section.

9.1

Residence

List all nonrented real property, including your primary or secondary residence, condominium or co-op apartment. Also include manufactured home ownership, regardless of whether you own the land on which it is located. Use the reverse to document major improvement projects.

Date Last Revised

Residence Information

Address

Residence Type

Parcel Number   Zoned

Title in the Name of

Purchase Date   Purchase Price $

Current Value $ Purchase Interest Rate %

Refinance Date 1   Amount of Refinance 1

Refinance Interest Rate 1   Refinance Fees Cost 1

Refinance Date 2   Amount of Refinance 2

Refinance Interest Rate 2   Refinance Fees Cost 2

Most Current Appraisal Date   Appraisal Value $

Location of Deeds and Documents

Mortgages

First Mortgage Held by   Loan No.

Mortgage Type

Address

Phone (   )   Fax (   )

E-Mail Address   WW Web Address

Payment Amount $ Payment Due Date

Approximate Amount Owed $ Date Due Full

Homeowner's Dues Amount $ Date(s) Due

Annual Property Insurance Amount $ Date(s) Due

Secured Line of Credit/Second Mortgage

Lending Institution   Account No.

Date Opened   Maximum Credit $

Approximate Current Balance

Interest Rate Tied to

Property Tax

Annual Tax Owed $

October 1st Payment Amount $

February 1st Payment Amount $

Local Property Tax Owed $ Date(s) Due

Location of Tax Receipts and Tax Forms

Helpful Hints
- Send all property tax payments and any important payments or documents by certified mail for proof of receipt.
- With proof of receipts, canceled checks and records, you can deduct from the capital gain upon the sale of the property all permanent improvements that add to the cost basis of the property.

  Examples of permanent improvements are: roof replacement, new hardwood floors, decks and landscaping. You cannot deduct routine upkeep, such as painting, from the selling price.

Examples of mortgage types are fixed-rate, adjustable rate, convertible, balloon, graduated payment, growing equity, shared application, buy-down and reverse mortgage, etc.

Three-hole punch and store any relevant information, property appraisal, contracts and leases after this form.

Residence

Continued

List only final cost of projects below.

Improvements

Description

_____

_____

Date Begun _____ Date Completed _____

Labor Costs $ _____ Material Costs $ _____ Total Costs $ _____

Location of Detailed Records _____

Location of Receipts _____

Description

_____

_____

Date Begun _____ Date Completed _____

Labor Costs $ _____ Material Costs $ _____ Total Costs $ _____

Location of Detailed Records _____

Location of Receipts _____

Description

_____

_____

Date Begun _____ Date Completed _____

Labor Costs $ _____ Material Costs $ _____ Total Costs $ _____

Location of Detailed Records _____

Location of Receipts _____

Description

_____

_____

Date Begun _____ Date Completed _____

Labor Costs $ _____ Material Costs $ _____ Total Costs $ _____

Location of Detailed Records _____

Location of Receipts _____

Description

_____

_____

Date Begun _____ Date Completed _____

Labor Costs $ _____ Material Costs $ _____ Total Costs $ _____

Location of Detailed Records _____

Location of Receipts _____

Three-hole punch and store any relevant information, property appraisal, contracts and leases after this form.

9.1

Residence

List all nonrented real property, including your primary or secondary residence, condominium or co-op apartment. Also include manufactured home ownership, regardless of whether you own the land on which it is located. Use the reverse to document major improvement projects.

Date Last Revised

Residence Information

Address

Residence Type

Parcel Number   Zoned

Title in the Name of

Purchase Date   Purchase Price $

Current Value $ Purchase Interest Rate %

Refinance Date 1   Amount of Refinance 1

Refinance Interest Rate 1   Refinance Fees Cost 1

Refinance Date 2   Amount of Refinance 2

Refinance Interest Rate 2   Refinance Fees Cost 2

Most Current Appraisal Date   Appraisal Value $

Location of Deeds and Documents

Mortgages

First Mortgage Held by   Loan No.

Mortgage Type

Address

Phone (   )   Fax (   )

E-Mail Address   WW Web Address

Payment Amount $ Payment Due Date

Approximate Amount Owed $ Date Due Full

Homeowner's Dues Amount $ Date(s) Due

Annual Property Insurance Amount $ Date(s) Due

Secured Line of Credit/Second Mortgage

Lending Institution   Account No.

Date Opened   Maximum Credit $

Approximate Current Balance

Interest Rate Tied to

Property Tax

Annual Tax Owed $

October 1st Payment Amount $

February 1st Payment Amount $

Local Property Tax Owed $ Date(s) Due

Location of Tax Receipts and Tax Forms

Helpful Hints
- Send all property tax payments and any important payments or documents by certified mail for proof of receipt.
- With proof of receipts, canceled checks and records, you can deduct from the capital gain upon the sale of the property all permanent improvements that add to the cost basis of the property.

  Examples of permanent improvements are: roof replacement, new hardwood floors, decks and landscaping. You cannot deduct routine upkeep, such as painting, from the selling price.

Examples of mortgage types are fixed-rate, adjustable rate, convertible, balloon, graduated payment, growing equity, shared application, buydown and reverse mortgage, etc.

Three-hole punch and store any relevant information, property appraisal, contracts and leases after this form.

Continued

List only final cost of projects below.

Improvements

Description

Date Begun   Date Completed

Labor Costs $ Material Costs $ Total Costs $

Location of Detailed Records

Location of Receipts

Description

Date Begun   Date Completed

Labor Costs $ Material Costs $ Total Costs $

Location of Detailed Records

Location of Receipts

Description

Date Begun   Date Completed

Labor Costs $ Material Costs $ Total Costs $

Location of Detailed Records

Location of Receipts

Description

Date Begun   Date Completed

Labor Costs $ Material Costs $ Total Costs $

Location of Detailed Records

Location of Receipts

Description

Date Begun   Date Completed

Labor Costs $ Material Costs $ Total Costs $

Location of Detailed Records

Location of Receipts

Three-hole punch and store any relevant information, property appraisal, contracts and leases after this form.

9.2

Income Property

List all rented real property. Use the reverse to document major improvement projects.

Date Last Revised

Property Information

Address

Parcel Number	Zoned

Title in the Name of

Purchase Date	Purchase Price $
Current Value $	Purchase Interest Rate %
Refinance Date 1	Amount of Refinance 1
Refinance Interest Rate 1	Refinance Fees Cost 1
Refinance Date 2	Amount of Refinance 2
Refinance Interest Rate 2	Refinance Fees Cost 2
Most Current Appraisal Date	Appraisal Value $

Location of Deeds and Documents

Mortgage

First Mortgage Held By	Loan No.
Address	
E-Mail Address	WW Web Address
Phone ( )	Fax ( )
Payment Amount $	Payment Due Date
Approximate Amount Owed $	Date Due Full
Monthly Income $	Outgo $
Manager's Name	Date(s) Due
Address	
Phone ( )	Fax ( )

Location of Tax Receipts and Tax Forms

Property Tax

Annual Tax Owed $

October 1st Payment Amount $

February 1st Payment Amount $

Local Property Tax Owed $	Date(s) Due

Location of Tax Receipts and Tax Forms

Helpful Hints

• Send all property tax payments and any important payments or documents by certified mail for proof of receipt.

• Always be sure to record property condition using photographs or videotapes before tenants move in, and again when they move out, as proof in case of need.

• With proof of receipts, canceled checks and records, you can deduct from the capital gain upon the sale of the property all permanent improvements that add to the cost basis of the property.

Examples of permanent improvements are roof replacement, new hardwood floors, decks and landscaping. You cannot deduct routine upkeep, such as painting, from the selling price.

Three-hole punch and store any relevant information, property appraisal, contracts and leases after this form.

Income Property

Continued

List only final cost of project below.

Improvements

Description

Date Began   Date Completed

Labor Costs $ Material Costs $ Total Costs $

Location of Detailed Records

Location of Receipts

Description

Date Began   Date Completed

Labor Costs $ Material Costs $ Total Costs $

Location of Detailed Records

Location of Receipts

Description

Date Began   Date Completed

Labor Costs $ Material Costs $ Total Costs $

Location of Detailed Records

Location of Receipts

Description

Date Began   Date Completed

Labor Costs $ Material Costs $ Total Costs $

Location of Detailed Records

Location of Receipts

Description

Date Began   Date Completed

Labor Costs $ Material Costs $ Total Costs $

Location of Detailed Records

Location of Receipts

Three-hole punch and store any relevant information, property appraisal, contracts and leases after this form.

10 Insurance

Remember to use a pencil on all forms.

PURPOSE

To fully protect yourself today from future unanticipated occurrences, you must hold insurance on your health, life, vehicle, property and other areas of your world.

Insurance is expensive and complex. Shop around and compare insurers and policies. Make sure you are getting adequate coverage for your needs and are not paying too much for your coverage.

Review your policies each year to make sure your policy is current with your needs.

The term *guaranteed renewal* is a vital provision to have in health insurance, especially as one gets older. Make sure the terms *guaranteed replacement* and *replacement cost of contents* are specified in your homeowner's insurance policy for current replacement value of your property.

The forms in this section are for your use in documenting all insurance policies you own for instant access to this information. Each form is designed with helpful hints, definitions and yearly insurance policy payment and pre-tax contribution tracking charts. These are helpful as a yearly reference when renewing your policies. At-a-glance, prior-year costs are there for comparison to the current year's quotes and charges.

These forms can also be invaluable for the one in charge, just in case.

HOW TO USE THESE FORMS

Fill out only those forms to which you relate and refer to them whenever insurance information is needed.

WHEN TO UPDATE

Update information as it occurs or once each year as your policies are renewed. When updating your new premium cost and before erasing the currently listed annual premium on your form, enter the currently listed amount in the prior years premiums chart on the bottom of each form. This provides excellent insurance cost tracking.

WHEN TO TOSS

Keep these forms for your lifetime. When information changes or a new policy is purchased, erase the old and enter the new in pencil.

OTHER FORMS TO KEEP

If you have documents or information not listed on the forms, three-hole punch and insert them in this section.

10.1

Health Insurance

List all health insurance policies, such as medical, hospital, dental, psychiatric and long-term care. Use a separate form for each policy held.

For annual contribution pretax expenses, refer to the back of this form.

Helpful Hints
- When mailing claims, be sure to keep a record of all claims and dates sent. Check off as claim is paid.

- Make sure each family member carries health card information at all times.

- The term *guaranteed renewal* is a vital provision to have in a health insurance policy, especially as one gets older.

To track premium costs, list current premium year and amount below prior to entering the new annual premium.

Three-hole punch and place after this form all additional health insurance information, current statement and policy booklets showing specific coverage details.

Date Last Revised

Policy Information

Name of Insured

Policy Company Name

Policy Company Address

E-Mail Address   WW Web Address

Phone (   )   Fax (   )

Policy No.   Group No.

Is the Policy a HMO, PPO, or an Indemnity?

Is the Policy Primary or Secondary?

Location of Identification Cards

Location of Policy

Insurance Agent's Company

Name

Address

E-Mail Address

Agent's Name

Phone (   )   Fax (   )

Premiums/Claims

Monthly Premium $ **Annual Premium $**

Method of Payment   Payment Due Date

Renewal Date

Send Payment To

Send Claim To

Phone (   )   Fax (   )

Health Benefits Adviser

Name

Address

E-Mail Address

Phone (   )   Fax (   )

Prior Years' Premiums

Year	Amount
	$

10.1

Health Insurance

Continued

If your employer has a pretax plan, record your participation below.

Date Last Revised

PreTax Health Payment Plan (FSA)

A *flexible spending account* (FSA) plan is a pretax health payment plan.

Is Your Contribution Made Monthly or Annually?		Amount $	
Prior Year Contributions	**Year**		**Amount**
		$	

PreTax Day Care Payment Plan

Is Your Contribution Made Monthly or Annually?		Amount $	
Prior Year Contributions	**Year**		**Amount**
		$	

Notes

_____

_____

_____

_____

_____

_____

_____

_____

_____

_____

_____

_____

_____

_____

_____

_____

_____

10.1 Health Insurance

List all health insurance policies, such as medical, hospital, dental, psychiatric and long-term care. Use a separate form for each policy held.

Date Last Revised

Policy Information

Name of Insured

Policy Company Name

Policy Company Address

E-Mail Address

WW Web Address

Phone (   )

Fax (   )

Policy No.

Group No.

Is the Policy a HMO, PPO, or an Indemnity?

Is the Policy Primary or Secondary?

Location of Identification Cards

Location of Policy

Insurance Agent's Company

Name

Address

E-Mail Address

Agent's Name

Phone (   )

Fax (   )

Premiums/Claims

Monthly Premium $

Annual Premium $

Method of Payment

Payment Due Date

Renewal Date

Send Payment To

Send Claim To

Phone (   )

Fax (   )

Health Benefits Adviser

Name

Address

E-Mail Address

Phone (   )

Fax (   )

Prior Years' Premiums

Year	Amount
	$

For annual contribution pretax expenses, refer to the back of this form.

Helpful Hints

• When mailing claims, be sure to keep a record of all claims and dates sent. Check off as claim is paid.

• Make sure each family member carries health card information at all times.

• The term *guaranteed renewal* is a vital provision to have in a health insurance policy, especially as one gets older.

To track premium costs, list current premium year and amount below prior to entering the new annual premium.

Three-hole punch and place after this form all additional health insurance information, current statement and policy booklets showing specific coverage details.

10.1

Health Insurance

Continued

If your employer has a pretax plan, record your participation below.

Date Last Revised

PreTax Health Payment Plan (FSA)

A *flexible spending account* (FSA) plan is a pretax health payment plan.

Is Your Contribution Made Monthly or Annually?   Amount $

Prior Year Contributions

Year	Amount
	$

PreTax Day Care Payment Plan

Is Your Contribution Made Monthly or Annually?   Amount $

Prior Year Contributions

Year	Amount
	$

Notes

_____

_____

_____

_____

_____

_____

_____

_____

_____

_____

_____

_____

_____

_____

_____

_____

_____

10.2 Disability Insurance

Complete only those sections or forms that pertain to you.

Helpful Hints
- Check your monthly budget to see how much additional income you would need in case of a long-term disability. Purchase your disability insurance accordingly.

- The best disability insurance policies provide benefits if you are unable to work at your *own* occupation rather than *any* general occupation.

Date Last Revised

Policy Information

Name of Insured

Policy Company Name

Policy Company Address

E-Mail Address   WW Web Address

Phone (   )   Fax (   )

Policy No.   Group No.

Location of Identification Cards

Location of Policy

Insurance Agent's Company

Name

Address

E-Mail Address

Agent's Name

Phone (   )   Fax (   )

Premiums/Claims

Monthly Premium $ Annual Premium $

Method of Payment   Payment Due Date

Renewal Date

Send Payment To

Send Claim To

Does coverage include your *own* occupation or *any* occupation?

Benefit Period   Benefit Amount $

Waiting Period

Policy Riders or Exclusion

Notes

Prior Years' Premiums

Year	Amount
	$

To track premium costs, list current premium year and amount here prior to entering the new annual premium.

Three-hole punch and place all additional disability insurance information, current statement and policy booklets showing specific coverage details after this form.

Disability Insurance

Continued

Date Last Revised

Policy Information

Name of Insured

Policy Company Name

Policy Company Address

E-Mail Address   WW Web Address

Phone (   )   Fax (   )

Policy No.   Group No.

Location of Identification Cards

Location of Policy

Insurance Agent's Company

Name

Address

E-Mail Address

Agent's Name

Phone (   )   Fax (   )

Premiums/Claims

Monthly Premium $ Annual Premium $

Method of Payment   Payment Due Date

Renewal Date

Send Payment To

Send Claim To

Does coverage include your *own* occupation or *any* occupation?

Benefit Period   Benefit Amount $

Waiting Period

Policy Riders or Exclusion

Notes

Helpful Hints

• Check your monthly budget to see how much additional income you would need in case of a long-term disability. Purchase your disability insurance accordingly.

• The best disability insurance policies provide benefits if you are unable to work at your *own* occupation rather than *any* general occupation.

Prior Years' Premiums

Year	Amount
	$

To track premium costs, list current premium year and amount here prior to entering the new annual premium.

Three-hole punch and place all additional disability insurance information, current statement and policy booklets showing specific coverage details after this form.

10.3 Long-Term Care Insurance

Long-term health care is care given for a chronic disability resulting from an illness, injury or decreased abilities due to aging. As life expectancy continues to climb, this type of insurance is becoming more important to have. List the long-term care policy you hold only if this form pertains to you.

Date Last Revised

Policy Information

Name of Insured

Policy Company Name

Policy Company Address

E-Mail Address   WW Web Address

Phone (   )   Fax (   )

Policy No.   Group No.

Location of Identification Cards

Location of Policy

Insurance Agent's Company

Name

Address

E-Mail Address

Agent's Name

Phone (   )   Fax (   )

Premiums/Claims

Monthly Premium $ **Annual Premium $**

Method of Payment   Payment Due Date

Renewal Date

Send Payment To

Address

Send Claim To

Phone (   )   Fax (   )

Health Benefits Adviser

Address

Phone (   )   Fax (   )

Notes

Helpful Hints
- Establishing a policy earlier (50-60) will lower your premium.

- Make sure the premiums on your policy will remain the same over the policy's life.

- Check with your state insurance department for a list of the companies selling long-term health care insurance in your state.

To track premium costs, list current premium year and amount here prior to entering the new annual premium.

Prior Years' Premiums

Year	Amount
	$

Three-hole punch and place all additional long-term care insurance information, current statement and policy booklets showing specific coverage details after this form.

Policy Coverage		Yes	No
	Activities of Daily Living (ADLs)		
	Cognitive Impairment		
	Disability vs. Medical Reimbursement		
	Elimination Period (EP)		
	Home Care Benefit		
	Nonforfeiture Benefit		
	Nursing Care Benefit		
	Pre-existing Conditions		

Make sure your policy covers most, if not all, of these items.

Terms To Know

Activities of Daily Living (ADLs): Functional ability such as feeding, bathing and dressing.

Cognitive Impairment: Mental illness impairments such as Alzheimer's Disease.

Disability vs. Medical Reimbursement: Disability allows more comprehensive coverage than medical which pays for actual service.

Elimination Period (EP): Time you must wait following the onset of an illness or injury before collecting benefit.

Home Care Benefit: Benefit paid for home-based care.

Nonforfeiture Benefit: Amount of benefit retained even when a policy is canceled.

Nursing Care Benefit: Benefit paid for care received in a nursing home.

Pre-existing Conditions: Provision that prevents coverage for conditions existing prior to purchasing the policy.

Notes _____

_____

_____

_____

_____

_____

_____

_____

10.3

Long-Term Care Insurance

Long-term health care is care given for a chronic disability resulting from an illness, injury or decreased abilities due to aging. As life expectancy continues to climb, this type of insurance is becoming more important to have. List the long-term care policy you hold only if this form pertains to you.

Date Last Revised

Policy Information

Name of Insured

Policy Company Name

Policy Company Address

E-Mail Address   WW Web Address

Phone (   )   Fax (   )

Policy No.   Group No.

Location of Identification Cards

Location of Policy

Insurance Agent's Company

Name

Address

E-Mail Address

Agent's Name

Phone (   )   Fax (   )

Premiums/Claims

Monthly Premium $ Annual Premium $

Method of Payment   Payment Due Date

Renewal Date

Send Payment To

Address

Send Claim To

Phone (   )   Fax (   )

Health Benefits Adviser

Address

Phone (   )   Fax (   )

Notes

Helpful Hints

- Establishing a policy earlier (50-60) will lower your premium.

- Make sure the premiums on your policy will remain the same over the policy's life.

- Check with your state insurance department for a list of the companies selling long-term health care insurance in your state.

To track premium costs, list current premium year and amount here prior to entering the new annual premium.

Prior Years' Premiums

Year	Amount
	$

Three-hole punch and place all additional long-term care insurance information, current statement and policy booklets showing specific coverage details after this form.

Long-Term Care Insurance

Continued

Policy Coverage		Yes	No
	Activities of Daily Living (ADLs)		
	Cognitive Impairment		
	Disability vs. Medical Reimbursement		
	Elimination Period (EP)		
	Home Care Benefit		
	Nonforfeiture Benefit		
	Nursing Care Benefit		
	Pre-existing Conditions		

Make sure your policy covers most, if not all, of these items.

Terms To Know

Activities of Daily Living (ADLs): Functional ability such as feeding, bathing and dressing.

Cognitive Impairment: Mental illness impairments such as Alzheimer's Disease.

Disability vs. Medical Reimbursement: Disability allows more comprehensive coverage than medical which pays for actual service.

Elimination Period (EP): Time you must wait following the onset of an illness or injury before collecting benefit.

Home Care Benefit: Benefit paid for home-based care.

Nonforfeiture Benefit: Amount of benefit retained even when a policy is canceled.

Nursing Care Benefit: Benefit paid for care received in a nursing home.

Pre-existing Conditions: Provision that prevents coverage for conditions existing prior to purchasing the policy.

Notes _____

_____

_____

_____

_____

_____

_____

_____

10.4　Life Insurance

Indicate whether whole life, universal, variable or term insurance. Use a separate form for each policy owned.

Date Last Revised

Policy Information

Name of Insured

Policy Owner

Policy No.   Type

Policy Location

Policy Company Name

Term insurance provides cash if you die. *Whole life, universal life* and *variable life insurance* are types of cash value combining a death benefit and an investment fund.

Address

E-Mail Address   WW Web Address

Phone (   )   Fax (   )

Insurance Agent's Company

Name

Address

E-Mail Address

Insurance Agent's Name

Phone (   )   Fax (   )

Premiums/Value

Monthly Premium $ Annual Premium $

Method of Payment   Payment Due Date

Send Payment To

Address

Renewal Date

Dividend Option

Total Cash Value $ Total Death Benefits $

Is There a Loan Against Your Policy?

Date Borrowed   Approximate Amount Owed $

Claims/Beneficiaries

Primary

Secondary

Claim Filing Procedures

To track premium costs, list current premium year and amount here prior to entering the new annual premium.

Prior Years' Premiums

Year	Amount
	$

Three-hole punch and place all additional life insurance information, current statement and policy booklets showing specific coverage details after this form.

Date Last Revised

Policy Information

Name of Insured

Policy Owner

Policy No.   Type

Policy Location

Policy Company Name

Address

E-Mail Address   WW Web Address

Phone (   )   Fax (   )

Insurance Agent's Company

Name

Address

E-Mail Address

Insurance Agent's Name

Phone (   )   Fax (   )

Premiums/Value

Monthly Premium $ Annual Premium $

Method of Payment   Payment Due Date

Send Payment To

Address

Renewal Date

Dividend Option

Total Cash Value $ Total Death Benefits $

Is There a Loan Against Your Policy?

Date Borrowed   Approximate Amount Owed $

Claims/Beneficiaries

Primary

Secondary

Claim Filing Procedures

Term insurance provides cash if you die. *Whole life, universal life* and *variable life insurance* are types of cash value combining a death benefit and an investment fund.

Prior Years' Premiums

Year	Amount
	$

To track premium costs, list current premium year and amount here prior to entering the new annual premium.

Three-hole punch and place all additional life insurance information, current statement and policy booklets showing specific coverage details after this form.

10.4   Life Insurance

Indicate whether whole life, universal, variable or term insurance. Use a separate form for each policy owned.

Term insurance provides cash if you die. *Whole life, universal life* and *variable life insurance* are types of cash value combining a death benefit and an investment fund.

Date Last Revised

Policy Information

Name of Insured

Policy Owner

Policy No.   Type

Policy Location

Policy Company Name

Address

E-Mail Address   WW Web Address

Phone (   )   Fax (   )

Insurance Agent's Company

Name

Address

E-Mail Address

Insurance Agent's Name

Phone (   )   Fax (   )

Premiums/Value

Monthly Premium $ Annual Premium $

Method of Payment   Payment Due Date

Send Payment To

Address

Renewal Date

Dividend Option

Total Cash Value $ Total Death Benefits $

Is There a Loan Against Your Policy?

Date Borrowed   Approximate Amount Owed $

Claims/Beneficiaries

Primary

Secondary

Claim Filing Procedures

To track premium costs, list current premium year and amount here prior to entering the new annual premium.

Prior Years' Premiums

Year	Amount
	$

Three-hole punch and place all additional life insurance information, current statement and policy booklets showing specific coverage details after this form.

Date Last Revised
_____

Policy Information

Name of Insured

Policy Owner

Policy No.   Type

Policy Location

Policy Company Name

Address

E-Mail Address   WW Web Address

Phone (   )   Fax (   )

Insurance Agent's Company

Name

Address

E-Mail Address

Insurance Agent's Name

Phone (   )   Fax (   )

Premiums/Value

Monthly Premium $ Annual Premium $

Method of Payment   Payment Due Date

Send Payment To

Address

Renewal Date

Dividend Option

Total Cash Value $ Total Death Benefits $

Is There a Loan Against Your Policy?

Date Borrowed   Approximate Amount Owed $

Claims/Beneficiaries

Primary

Secondary

Claim Filing Procedures

Term insurance provides cash if you die. _Whole life, universal life_ and _variable life insurance_ are types of cash value combining a death benefit and an investment fund.

Prior Years' Premiums

Year	Amount
	$

To track premium costs, list current premium year and amount here prior to entering the new annual premium.

Three-hole punch and place all additional life insurance information, current statement and policy booklets showing specific coverage details after this form.

10.5

Vehicle Insurance

Complete a separate form for each policy held and only those categories that apply to you.

You may be required to insure boats, motorcycles, motor homes and other types of vehicles with specialty insurance companies. For specific insurance requirements within your state, check with your insurance agent or your local Department of Motor Vehicles.

Date Last Revised

Policy Information

Policy Company Name

Address

E-Mail Address   WW Web Address

Phone (   )   Fax (   )

Policy No.   Policy Location

Insurance Agent's Company

Name

Address

E-Mail Address

Insurance Agent's Name

Phone (   )   Fax (   )

Premiums

Monthly Premium $ **Annual Premium $**

Method of Payment

Payment Due Date   Renewal Date

Refer to your policy for details of insurance policy coverage amounts ie., liability, comprehensive.

Vehicles Insured

Make   Model   Year

Body Type   Vehicle ID No.

License No.   Owned or Leased?

Name(s) of Insured(s) on This Vehicle   Towing Card No.

List Extended Warranties

Include all vehicles insured on this policy.

Make   Model   Year

Body Type   Vehicle ID No.

License No.   Owned or Leased?

Name(s) of Insured(s) on This Vehicle   Towing Card No.

List Extended Warranties

To track premium costs, list current premium year and amount here prior to entering the new annual premium.

Prior Years' Premiums

Year	Amount
	$

Three-hole punch and place all additional vehicle insurance information, current coverage statement and policy booklets showing specific coverage details after this form.

Vehicles Insured *Continued*

Make   Model   Year

Body Type   Vehicle ID No.

License No.   Owned or Leased?

Name(s) of Insured(s) on This Vehicle   Towing Card No.

List Extended Warranties

Make   Model   Year

Body Type   Vehicle ID No.

License No.   Owned or Leased?

Name(s) of Insured(s) on This Vehicle   Towing Card No.

List Extended Warranties

Make   Model   Year

Body Type   Vehicle ID No.

License No.   Owned or Leased?

Name(s) of Insured(s) on This Vehicle   Towing Card No.

List Extended Warranties

Make   Model   Year

Body Type   Vehicle ID No.

License No.   Owned or Leased?

Name(s) of Insured(s) on This Vehicle   Towing Card No.

List Extended Warranties

Make   Model   Year

Body Type   Vehicle ID No.

License No.   Owned or Leased?

Name(s) of Insured(s) on This Vehicle   Towing Card No.

List Extended Warranties

Vehicle Towing Service Used   Phone (   )

Yearly Cost $ Card Expiration Date

Include all vehicles insured on this policy.

Prior Years' Premiums

Year	Amount
	$

To track premium costs, list current premium year and amount here prior to entering the new annual premium.

Three-hole punch and place all additional vehicle insurance information, current coverage statement and policy booklets showing specific coverage details after this form.

10.6 Homeowner's Insurance

Complete a separate form for each property you own or lease. Include any nonrented second home, vacation home, co-op apartment or condominium. Remember to use a pencil so you can update information as it occurs.

Date Last Revised

Policy Information

Property Address

Policy in the Name of

Policy No.   Policy Location

Policy Company Name

Address

E-Mail Address   WW Web Address

Phone (   )   Fax (   )

Insurance Agent's Company

Name

Address

E-Mail Address

Insurance Agent's Name

Phone (   )   Fax (   )

Premiums/Claims

Monthly Premium $ Annual Premium $

Method of Payment

Payment Due Date   Renewal Date

Send Payment to

Address

Phone (   )   Fax (   )

Amount of Property Coverage $ Amount of Content Coverage $

Amount of Liability Coverage $ Deductible $

Amount of Scheduled Items $ Amount of Umbrella Liability $

Amount of Disaster Coverage $

Claim Filing Procedures

Prior Years' Premiums

Year	Amount
	$

Helpful Hints

- Take videotapes and photographs of all personal possessions. Keep these in a fire-proof box or in a safe place away from home.

- Make sure the terms *guaranteed replacement* and *replacement cost of contents* are specified on your policy for current replacement value.

- Try to purchase extra disaster insurance pertaining to your area whenever possible.

Refer to Form 8.2, "Tangible Assets Inventory," and Form 9.1, "Residence," for inventory lists and appraisals.

To track premium costs, list current premium year and amount here prior to entering the new annual premium.

Three-hole punch and place all additional homeowner's insurance information, current statement and policy booklets showing specific coverage details after this form.

Date Last Revised _____

Policy Information

Property Address

Policy in the Name of _____

Policy No. _____ Policy Location _____

Policy Company Name

Address _____

E-Mail Address _____ WW Web Address _____

Phone ( ) _____ Fax ( ) _____

Insurance Agent's Company

Name _____

Address _____

E-Mail Address _____

Insurance Agent's Name _____

Phone ( ) _____ Fax ( ) _____

Premiums/Claims

Monthly Premium $ _____ Annual Premium $ _____

Method of Payment _____

Payment Due Date _____ Renewal Date _____

Send Payment to

Address _____

Phone ( ) _____ Fax ( ) _____

Amount of Property Coverage $ _____ Amount of Content Coverage $ _____

Amount of Liability Coverage $ _____ Deductible $ _____

Amount of Scheduled Items $ _____ Amount of Umbrella Liability $ _____

Amount of Disaster Coverage $ _____

Claim Filing Procedures

_____

_____

_____

_____

_____

Prior Years' Premiums

Year	Amount
_____	$ _____
_____	_____
_____	_____
_____	_____

Helpful Hints

- Take videotapes and photographs of all personal possessions. Keep these in a fire-proof box or in a safe place away from home.

- Make sure the terms *guaranteed replacement* and *Replacement Cost of Contents* are specified on your policy for current replacement value.

- Try to purchase extra disaster insurance pertaining to your area whenever possible.

Refer to Form 8.2, "Tangible Assets Inventory," and Form 9.1, "Residence," for inventory lists and appraisals.

To track premium costs, list current premium year and amount here prior to entering the new annual premium.

Three-hole punch and place all additional homeowner's insurance information, current statement and policy booklets showing specific coverage details after this form.

10.6

Homeowner's Insurance

Complete a separate form for each property you own or lease. Include any nonrented second home, vacation home, co-op apartment or condominium. Remember to use a pencil so you can update information as it occurs.

Date Last Revised

Policy Information

Property Address

Policy in the Name of

Policy No.   Policy Location

Policy Company Name

Address

E-Mail Address   WW Web Address

Phone (   )   Fax (   )

Insurance Agent's Company

Name

Address

E-Mail Address

Insurance Agent's Name

Phone (   )   Fax (   )

Premiums/Claims

Monthly Premium $ Annual Premium $

Method of Payment

Payment Due Date   Renewal Date

Send Payment to

Address

Phone (   )   Fax (   )

Amount of Property Coverage $ Amount of Content Coverage $

Amount of Liability Coverage $ Deductible $

Amount of Scheduled Items $ Amount of Umbrella Liability $

Amount of Disaster Coverage $

Claim Filing Procedures

Prior Years' Premiums

Year	Amount
	$
	$
	$

Refer to Form 8.2, "Tangible Assets Inventory," and Form 9.1, "Residence," for inventory lists and appraisals.

Helpful Hints

- Take videotapes and photographs of all personal possessions. Keep these in a fire-proof box or in a safe place away from home.

- Make sure the terms *guaranteed replacement* and *Replacement Cost of Contents* are specified on your policy for current replacement value.

- Try to purchase extra disaster insurance pertaining to your area whenever possible.

To track premium costs, list current premium year and amount here prior to entering the new annual premium.

Three-hole punch and place all additional homeowner's insurance information, current statement and policy booklets showing specific coverage details after this form.

Date Last Revised _____

Policy Information

Property Address

Policy in the Name of _____

Policy No. _____   Policy Location _____

Policy Company Name

Address _____

E-Mail Address _____   WW Web Address _____

Phone ( ) _____   Fax ( ) _____

Insurance Agent's Company

Name _____

Address _____

E-Mail Address _____

Insurance Agent's Name _____

Phone ( ) _____   Fax ( ) _____

Premiums/Claims

Monthly Premium $ _____   Annual Premium $ _____

Method of Payment _____

Payment Due Date _____   Renewal Date _____

Send Payment to

Address _____

Phone ( ) _____   Fax ( ) _____

Amount of Property Coverage $ _____   Amount of Content Coverage $ _____

Amount of Liability Coverage $ _____   Deductible $ _____

Amount of Scheduled Items $ _____   Amount of Umbrella Liability $ _____

Amount of Disaster Coverage $ _____

Claim Filing Procedures

_____

_____

_____

_____

_____

Prior Years' Premiums

Year	Amount
_____	$ _____
_____	_____
_____	_____
_____	_____

Helpful Hints

- Take videotapes and photographs of all personal possessions. Keep these in a fire-proof box or in a safe place away from home.

- Make sure the terms *guaranteed replacement* and *Replacement Cost of Contents* are specified on your policy for current replacement value.

- Try to purchase extra disaster insurance pertaining to your area whenever possible.

Refer to Form 8.2, "Tangible Assets Inventory," and Form 9.1, "Residence," for inventory lists and appraisals.

To track premium costs, list current premium year and amount here prior to entering the new annual premium.

Three-hole punch and place all additional homeowner's insurance information, current statement and policy booklets showing specific coverage details after this form.

10.7

Renter's Insurance

Complete this form if you rent an apartment, condominium or home. Remember to use a pencil so you can update information as it occurs.

Date Last Revised

Policy Information

Property Address

Policy in the Name of

Policy No.   Policy Location

Policy Company Name

Address

E-Mail Address   WW Web Address

Phone (   )   Fax (   )

Insurance Agent's Company

Name

Address

E-Mail Address

Insurance Agent's Name

Phone (   )   Fax (   )

Premiums/Claims

Monthly Premium $ **Annual Premium $**

Method of Payment

Payment Due Date   Renewal Date

Send Payments to

Phone (   )   Fax (   )

Amount of Content Coverage $

Amount of Liability Coverage $ Deductible $

Other Coverage   Amount $

Claim Filing Procedures

Prior Years' Premiums

Year	Amount
	$

Refer to Form 8.2, "Tangible Assets Inventory," for inventory lists and appraisals.

Helpful Hints
- Take videotapes and photographs of all personal possessions. Keep these in a fire-proof box or in a safe place away from home.

- If you rent, it is a good idea to have liability coverage on your renter's insurance policy in addition to personal property insurance. This increases your protection from liability for harm to others or their property.

To track premium costs, list current premium year and amount here prior to entering the new annual premium.

Three-hole punch and place all additional renter's insurance information, current statements and policy booklets showing specific coverage details after this form.

Renter's Insurance

Continued

Date Last Revised

Policy Information

Property Address

Policy in the Name of

Policy No.   Policy Location

Policy Company Name

Address

E-Mail Address   WW Web Address

Phone (   )   Fax (   )

Insurance Agent's Company

Name

Address

E-Mail Address

Insurance Agent's Name

Phone (   )   Fax (   )

Premiums/Claims

Monthly Premium $ **Annual Premium $**

Method of Payment

Payment Due Date   Renewal Date

Send Payments to

Phone (   )   Fax (   )

Amount of Content Coverage $

Amount of Liability Coverage $ Deductible $

Other Coverage   Amount $

Claim Filing Procedures

Prior Years' Premiums

To track premium costs, list current premium year and amount here prior to entering the new annual premium.

Year	Amount
	$

Three-hole punch and place all additional renter's insurance information, current statements and policy booklets showing specific coverage details after this form.

10.8

Income Property Insurance

Complete a separate form for each property you own and rent or lease. Remember to use a pencil so you can update information as it occurs.

Helpful Hints
- Always be sure to record property condition using photographs or video-tape before tenants move in and again when they move out, in case you need proof.

- Make sure the terms *guaranteed replacement* and *replacement cost of contents* are specified on your policy for current replacement value.

Refer to Form 9.1, "Residence," for appraisals and inventory details. Refer to Form 9.2, "Income Property," for income property details.

Date Last Revised

Policy Information

Property Address

Policy in the Name of

Policy No.   Policy Location

Policy Company Name

Address

E-Mail Address   WW Web Address

Phone (   )   Fax (   )

Insurance Agent's Company

Name

Address

E-Mail Address

Insurance Agent's Name

Phone (   )   Fax (   )

Premiums/Claims

Monthly Premium $ **Annual Premium $**

Method of Payment

Payment Due Date   Renewal Date

Send Payments to

Phone (   )   Fax (   )

Amount of Property Coverage $ Amount of Content Coverage $

Amount of Liability Coverage $ Deductible $

Amount of Scheduled Items $ Amount of Umbrella Liability $

Amount of Disaster Coverage $

Claim Filing Procedures

To track premium costs, list current premium year and amount here prior to entering the new annual premium.

Prior Years' Premiums

Year	Amount
	$

Three-hole punch and place all additional property insurance information, current statement and policy booklets showing specific coverage details after this form.

Income Property Insurance

Continued

Date Last Revised

Policy Information

Property Address

Policy in the Name of

Policy No.   Policy Location

Policy Company Name

Address

E-Mail Address   WW Web Address

Phone (   )   Fax (   )

Insurance Agent's Company

Name

Address

E-Mail Address

Insurance Agent's Name

Phone (   )   Fax (   )

Premiums/Claims

Monthly Premium $ **Annual Premium $**

Method of Payment

Payment Due Date   Renewal Date

Send Payments to

Phone (   )   Fax (   )

Amount of Property Coverage $ Amount of Content Coverage $

Amount of Liability Coverage $ Deductible $

Amount of Scheduled Items $ Amount of Umbrella Liability $

Amount of Disaster Coverage $

Claim Filing Procedures

Prior Years' Premiums

Year	Amount
	$

11 Last Instructions

Remember to use a pencil on all forms, except Form 11.5.

PURPOSE

The most difficult thing those left behind must do is to make those very important last decisions for you. So the most helpful thing you can do for your family, spouse, care-giver or those left in charge, is to be prepared and make your own wishes known.

It is vital that you and your spouse each have prepared and signed a current will, special bequests, current living will, health care power of attorney and durable powers of attorney forms. In addition, you should make sure that all last instructions are current and all forms in this book are updated. When you have finished, you can relax knowing that your life is in order and that you have made the job much easier for those who must take charge.

This section provides full definitions of powers of attorney, prearranged funerals and organ donor programs and a **"What To Do at Time of Death"** checklist. For your reference, this checklist provides a full list of arrangements that must be carried out immediately after and up through the first six months. Once you review these lists and definitions, you will see how important it is to keep your records organized and current—especially for the one left in charge.

HOW TO USE THESE FORMS

These forms have been designed to guide you through this process. Fill out only those forms and lines that apply to you.

WHEN TO UPDATE

Update information as it changes. Be sure to update your wills as your financial status or wishes change and to destroy any outdated wills immediately.

Be sure those "to be in charge" know the contents and location of your will, location of all powers of attorney for immediate access and the location of this kit.

WHEN TO TOSS

These forms are intended to be kept for your lifetime.

OTHER FORMS TO KEEP

If you have documents or information not listed on the forms, three-hole punch and insert them in this section or indicate their location on the related form.

11.1 Last Instructions Preparation

To be certain that your wishes are carried out in the event of your incapacity, you must have made arrangements in advance using the appropriate documents. Included below are available resources and definitions to make your preparation more thorough.

Laws governing durable power of attorney, health care power of attorney and living wills vary greatly from state to state. Be certain to consult an attorney in your state of current residence regarding the state laws and to obtain the necessary forms you will need. These forms are also available in most stationery stores or write National Council for the Right To Die (200 Varick Street, 10th Floor, New York, NY 10014; 212-366-5540). When traveling, consider carrying copies of one or all of these forms with you.

POWER OF ATTORNEY

This gives the individual you've named the right to act on your behalf only while you are competent; e.g., the right to sign documents on your behalf. When you become incompetent or die, the power of attorney given to that individual ceases.

DURABLE POWER OF ATTORNEY

A durable power of attorney is a document authorizing another person to act in your behalf as your legal representative when signing legal papers, transferring funds or performing a number of other legally binding tasks when you become incapacitated.

The person you name in your durable power of attorney *while you are competent* can act for you only when you are incompetent. Your durable power of attorney can also cover health care issues, or you can use a separate power of attorney form.

DURABLE POWER OF ATTORNEY FOR HEALTH CARE

This identifies the person whom you wish to make medical decisions for you if you are unable to do so. Only that person who holds *legal* durable power of attorney for health care can make medical decisions for you. In conjunction with the health care power of attorney, you can and should sign a living will.

LIVING WILL

This document declares that you do not wish to be kept alive by extraordinary artificial life-support systems and authorizes doctors and named relatives to disconnect any equipment keeping you alive. It is activated when you become mentally or physically incapacitated.

PREARRANGED FUNERAL

If you choose to plan and prepay your funeral arrangements, an up-front fee is required to cover all expenses. The money earmarked specifically for this purpose can be placed in the following types of trust funds.

- *Totten Trust:* individual savings plan controlled by you for the funeral. Upon death, money is immediately released for the funeral.
- *Regulated Trust:* money is invested by the funeral home or cemetery to pay for the burial. You have no access to the money and any extra monies are retained by the funeral home or cemetery after the funeral.

ORGAN DONATION CARDS

Always carry your donation card in your wallet in order to guarantee your wishes are honored. To obtain a card, contact The Living Bank (P.O. Box 6725, Houston, TX 77265-6725; 713-528-2971).

For information on donating your body to medical science, contact the National Anatomical Service (800-727-0700).

11.2

What To Do at Time of Death

When needed, this checklist can be invaluable. Place a check on each line below as each task is completed.

To My Heirs and Survivors

Below are steps to follow at the time of my death. When you need information relating to my/our records, refer to Form 1.2, **"Location of Documents and Records,"** in this kit for the form number where it can be found.

Immediately	Completed?	Date
Make all funeral arrangements: service, burial.		
Send obituary notices.		
Notify friends and relatives.		
Authorize donation of body parts.		
Contact medical school for body bequeathal.		
Keep list of all expressions of sympathy		
Arrange after-service gathering.		
Make sure survivor(s) have access to emergency funds.		
Open new checking account in your name.		
Obtain 20 certified copies of death certificate.		
Other		
Other		
Other		

First Month		
Arrange all checking and savings accounts in your name. *Note:* Keep accounts separate from probate proceedings.		
Establish a new "estate" bank account in deceased's name. *Note:* Holds funds received from benefits, available after probate, helps pay taxes.		
Notify insurance companies, file for benefits. *Note:* Life, medical, health, disability, accident, vehicle, residence, travel.		
Review auto insurance policy. *Note:* May carry additional insurance benefits.		
Apply for benefits from Social Security, pension, workers' compensation, veteran's benefits.		
Notify deceased's employer for benefits due.		
Meet with deceased's attorney to begin probate proceedings. *Note:* For estates valued over $600,000. Take original will & kit.		
Notify accountant. *Note:* Take Kit and copies of past two years' tax returns to look for assets in records.		
Enter safe-deposit box for important documents.		
Notify all IRA and Keogh accounts.		
Notify stockbroker(s). *Note:* Remove decedent's name from joint ownership of owned securities.		
Check medical policies for claim filing time restrictions.		
Other		
Other		
Other		

Continued on back

What To Do at Time of Death

Continued

First Two Months	Completed ?	Date
Make sure attorney files the will.		
Have accountant file federal estate and inheritance tax returns.		
Select a financial adviser.		
Transfer home and all jointly owned real estate titles.		
Transfer all car titles.		
Transfer all insurance policies.		
Change utilities to your own name.		
Change telephone listings.		
Remove deceased's name where listed as beneficiary.		
Revise your own will.		
Make sure your medical insurance is adequate.		
Notify all creditors		
Other		
Other		
Other		

First Six Months		
Review all forms in this book. Make sure they're current.		
Create a new budget.		
Review all insurance needs. Make sure they're current.		
Begin a new investment plan.		
If an executor is involved, make sure he or she is working for YOU.		
Other		
Other		
Other		

Notes _____

_____

_____

_____

_____

_____

_____

_____

11.3

Final Arrangements

Complete only those sections or pages that pertain to you. Each "Final Arrangements" form applies to one individual.

For more on prearranged funeral expense information and definitions, refer to Form 11.1 "Last Instructions Preparation," in this section.

Date Last Revised

Name

Location of Burial Plot

Location of Burial Plot Deed

Contact   Phone (   )

Plot No.   Prepaid?

Amount Paid $ Amount Due $

Payment Due Date

Do You Own Burial Insurance?

Issuing Company

Policy Number

Address

Phone (   )

Coverage Amount or Benefit $

Have You Made Funeral Arrangements?   Prepaid?

Amount Prepaid $ Trust Fund Type

Funeral Home

Contact   Phone (   )

Address

Notes

Three-hole punch and store any relevant information after this form. Include an obituary notice if desired.

Final Arrangements

Continued

Use this page to write in your own words any additional instructions, such as burial or cremation, donation of organs or body parts, names of pall bearers, casket or tombstone desires, funeral or memorial arrangements, or who is to officiate.

Additional Instructions

_____

_____

_____

Refer to Form 11.1, "Last
Instructions Preparation,"
in this section for information on donation of organ
and body parts.

_____

_____

_____

_____

_____

_____

_____

_____

_____

People To Contact upon My Death

You might include family,
friends, executor, people
to care for children, em-
ployer, religious counselor,
business associates, attorney, landlord, banker,
mortgage holder and
others.

Name _____ Phone ( )_____

Address _____

Relationship _____

Name _____ Phone ( )_____

Address _____

Relationship _____

Name _____ Phone ( )_____

Address _____

Relationship _____

Name _____ Phone ( )_____

Address _____

Relationship _____

Three-hole punch and
store any relevant
information after this form.
Include an obituary notice
if desired.

11.3   Final Arrangements

Complete only those sections or pages that pertain to you. Each "Final Arrangements" form applies to one individual.

For more on prearranged funeral expense information and definitions, refer to Form 11.1 "Last Instructions Preparation," in this section.

Date Last Revised

Name

Location of Burial Plot

Location of Burial Plot Deed

Contact   Phone (   )

Plot No.   Prepaid?

Amount Paid $ Amount Due $

                                          Payment Due Date

Do You Own Burial Insurance?

Issuing Company

Policy Number

Address

Phone (   )

Coverage Amount or Benefit $

Have You Made Funeral Arrangements?   Prepaid?

Amount Prepaid $ Trust Fund Type

Funeral Home

Contact   Phone (   )

Address

Notes

Three-hole punch and store any relevant information after this form. Include an obituary notice if desired.

11.3

Final Arrangements

Continued

Use this page to write in your own words any additional instructions, such as burial or cremation, donation of organs or body parts, names of pall bearers, casket or tombstone desires, funeral or memorial arrangements, or who is to officiate.

Additional Instructions

Refer to Form 11.1, "Last Instructions Preparation," in this section for information on donation of organ and body parts.

People To Contact upon My Death

You might include family, friends, executor, people to care for children, employer, religious counselor, business associates, attorney, landlord, banker, mortgage holder and others.

Name _____ Phone ( )

Address _____

Relationship _____

Name _____ Phone ( )

Address _____

Relationship _____

Name _____ Phone ( )

Address _____

Relationship _____

Name _____ Phone ( )

Address _____

Relationship _____

Three-hole punch and store any relevant information after this form. Include an obituary notice if desired.

11.4

Copies of Wills

Complete only those sections or forms that pertain to you.

Date Last Revised

Name

Date of Most Recent Will

Location of Will

Executor's Name   Phone (   )

Address

People Holding Copies of Will

Name   Phone (   )

Address

Relationship

Name   Phone (   )

Address

Relationship

Name   Phone (   )

Address

Relationship

Name   Phone (   )

Address

Relationship

Name   Phone (   )

Address

Relationship

Name   Phone (   )

Address

Relationship

Name   Phone (   )

Address

Relationship

Name   Phone (   )

Address

Relationship

Helpful Hints

Be sure to dispose of all outdated wills.

Refer to Form 11.1, "Last Instructions Preparation," in this section for the definition of and how to obtain a living will form.

Photocopy, three-hole punch and store a copy of your will after this form.

Copies of Wills

Continued

Notes

_____

_____

_____

_____

_____

_____

_____

_____

_____

_____

_____

_____

_____

_____

_____

_____

_____

_____

_____

_____

_____

_____

_____

_____

_____

_____

Photocopy, three-hole
punch and store a copy of
your will after this form.

11.4

Copies of Wills

Complete only those sections or forms that pertain to you.

Date Last Revised

Name

Date of Most Recent Will

Location of Will

Executor's Name   Phone (   )

Address

Helpful Hints
Be sure to dispose of all outdated wills.

Refer to Form 11.1, "Last Instructions Preparation," in this section for the definition of and how to obtain a living will form.

People Holding Copies of Will

Name   Phone (   )

Address

Relationship

Name   Phone (   )

Address

Relationship

Name   Phone (   )

Address

Relationship

Name   Phone (   )

Address

Relationship

Name   Phone (   )

Address

Relationship

Name   Phone (   )

Address

Relationship

Name   Phone (   )

Address

Relationship

Name   Phone (   )

Address

Relationship

Photocopy, three-hole punch and store a copy of your will after this form.

Copies of Wills

Continued

Notes

_____

_____

_____

_____

_____

_____

_____

_____

_____

_____

_____

_____

_____

_____

_____

_____

_____

_____

_____

_____

_____

_____

_____

_____

_____

_____

_____

_____

_____

Photocopy, three-hole
punch and store a copy of
your will after this form.

11.5

Special Bequests

A *bequest* is a gift of personal property by will. Complete this form to designate specific items that you wish to give to specific individuals, for example, jewelry, silver, art, photography or other favorite possessions.

Complete this form using a pen.

Date Last Revised

Name

Item	For Whom	Bequested in Will? Yes/No

This special bequests form is for reference only. To be legally binding, a specific special bequests list should be included in your current and signed will.

Helpful Hints
If bequested assets are also included in custodial accounts refer to Form 7.1, "Custodial Accounts."

Three-hole punch and store any relevant information after this form.

Special Bequests

A *bequest* is a gift of personal property by will. Complete this form to designate specific items that you wish to give to specific individuals, for example, jewelry, silver, art, photography or other favorite possessions.

Complete this form using a pen.

Date Last Revised
_____

Name

Item	For Whom	Bequested in Will? Yes/No

This special bequests form is for reference only. To be legally binding, a specific special bequests list should be included in your current and signed will.

Helpful Hints
If bequested assets are also included in custodial accounts refer to Form 7.1, "Custodial Accounts."

Three-hole punch and store any relevant information after this form.

12 Income Tax Records

Remember to use a pencil on all forms.

PURPOSE

Taxes probably represent one of your largest expenditures. By keeping all organized receipts and records for tax related items during the year, you will help yourself save money at tax time.

Each time you apply for a loan, line of credit or various investments, you may need to present copies of the past two years income tax returns.

This section is designed to hold photocopies of the past two years' income tax returns for easy access. As a rule, you receive two original sets of federal and state income tax returns from your accountant, one to be sent and one to keep for your records. Place your original copies in a fire-proof file, box or safe. Many times you must present the original return; therefore, it must be in a safe place.

HOW TO USE THESE FORMS

List the location of all original returns on Form 12.1, **"Copies of Past Two Years' Income Tax Returns."** Three-hole punch and insert photocopies of the returns behind Form 12.1 if you are using the loose-leaf notebook format. If you are using this kit or you wish not to keep copies of your income tax returns in your loose-leaf binder kit, indicate where all originals and photocopies can be located.

WHEN TO UPDATE

Update information as it changes. Insert income tax return when completed and taxes have been filed. You should keep all returns at least seven years. Once the return is outdated for this kit (at the end of the second year), remove and store safely.

Be sure to indicate where all past returns, related canceled checks and receipts are located on Form 1.2, **"Location of Documents and Records."**

WHEN TO TOSS

These forms are intended to be kept for your lifetime.

OTHER FORMS TO KEEP

If you have documents or information not listed on the forms, three-hole punch and insert them in this section or indicate their location on the appropriate form.

12.1

Copies of Past Two Years' Income Tax Returns

Photocopy, three-hole punch and store income tax returns for the past two years after this form.

Date Last Revised

List the Years of Income Tax Returns Inserted After This Form

Location of All Original Returns

All Original Returns Kept Back to What Year

Notes

Helpful Hints

• Keep original documents, canceled checks and receipts in a secure location, safe from natural disasters, thefts and accidental destruction or loss.

• A tax audit normally occurs one to three years after your last filing date. In the event of an audit, you will be required to produce original receipts and canceled checks.

• If you have underreported your income by 25 percent or more, the IRS has six years to audit. And if you don't file or file a false return, they have forever.

• The IRS recommends that you keep canceled checks and receipts for at least seven years.

Three-hole punch and store any relevant information after this form.

Appendix: References

Remember to use a pencil on each form.

PURPOSE

To be totally organized, you should keep a current list of whom to contact in case of renewal, cancelation or loss of all credit cards. In addition, a current listing of all subscriptions, amounts paid, due dates and cancelation numbers kept for either yourself or the "one in charge" is always helpful.

This section contains forms to list all credit cards and subscriptions held. Additionally, it contains Appendix A, **"Helpful Agency Listings,"** on which to log all federal bureau phone numbers and addresses you have called or may need in the future.

HOW TO USE THESE FORMS

Fill out only those forms that apply to you. As you find a need for local or federal bureau or agency information, list on Appendix A for future reference. Appendix B, **"Credit/Debit Card Index,"** can be very helpful as an instant reference to your card numbers if lost or if you simply need a card number quickly.

WHEN TO UPDATE

Update as information changes, a subscription is canceled or purchased or a credit card is changed, canceled or acquired.

WHEN TO TOSS

These forms are intended for you to keep for your lifetime.

OTHER FORMS TO KEEP

If you have additional reference information you wish to keep, three-hole punch and insert it in this section or indicate the location on the appropriate form.

A

Helpful Agency Listings

As questions arise regarding Social Security, the Better Business Bureau, IRS, social services or unclaimed property inquiries, etc., which require phone numbers and addresses in your state or nationally, list those numbers below, as acquired, for future reference.

Date Last Revised

Helpful Hints
For specific agency listings, refer to local or (800) phone books. Local and (800) information operators can also be helpful.

Type of Agency

Name of Agency

Contact at Agency

Address

E-Mail Address

Phone (   )   Fax (   )

Type of Agency

Name of Agency

Contact at Agency

Address

E-Mail Address

Phone (   )   Fax (   )

Type of Agency

Name of Agency

Contact at Agency

Address

E-Mail Address

Phone (   )   Fax (   )

Type of Agency

Name of Agency

Contact at Agency

Address

E-Mail Address

Phone (   )   Fax (   )

Type of Agency

Name of Agency

Contact at Agency

Address

E-Mail Address

Phone (   )   Fax (   )

Helpful Agency Listings

Continued

Type of Agency

Name of Agency

Contact at Agency

Address

E-Mail Address

Phone (   )   Fax (   )

Type of Agency

Name of Agency

Contact at Agency

Address

E-Mail Address

Phone (   )   Fax (   )

Type of Agency

Name of Agency

Contact at Agency

Address

E-Mail Address

Phone (   )   Fax (   )

Type of Agency

Name of Agency

Contact at Agency

Address

E-Mail Address

Phone (   )   Fax (   )

Type of Agency

Name of Agency

Contact at Agency

Address

E-Mail Address

Phone (   )   Fax (   )

B Credit/Debit Card Index

List all cards such as car rental, bank guarantee, airline, gasoline, credit and debit cards. Photocopy and take the copy with you when you travel. Keep another copy in your safe deposit box or some other safe place. The original should remain in this kit.

Date Last Revised

Issued by	Card No.
Expiration Date	Lost Card Phone ( )
Name(s) on Card	

Helpful Hints
- Set up a system for saving all receipts of debit card purchases for accurate record-keeping purposes. Keep them until you verify purchase amounts on monthly statements or item is returned.
- If the purchased item is tax deductible, keep the receipt as proof for seven years.

Issued by	Card No.
Expiration Date	Lost Card Phone ( )
Name(s) on Card	

Issued by	Card No.
Expiration Date	Lost Card Phone ( )
Name(s) on Card	

Issued by	Card No.
Expiration Date	Lost Card Phone ( )
Name(s) on Card	

Issued by	Card No.
Expiration Date	Lost Card Phone ( )
Name(s) on Card	

Issued by	Card No.
Expiration Date	Lost Card Phone ( )
Name(s) on Card	

Issued by	Card No.
Expiration Date	Lost Card Phone ( )
Name(s) on Card	

Issued by	Card No.
Expiration Date	Lost Card Phone ( )
Name(s) on Card	

Three-hole punch and store any relevant information after this form.

Credit/Debit Card Index

Continued

Issued by	Card No.
Expiration Date	Lost Card Phone ( )
Name(s) on Card	

Issued by	Card No.
Expiration Date	Lost Card Phone ( )
Name(s) on Card	

Issued by	Card No.
Expiration Date	Lost Card Phone ( )
Name(s) on Card	

Issued by	Card No.
Expiration Date	Lost Card Phone ( )
Name(s) on Card	

Issued by	Card No.
Expiration Date	Lost Card Phone ( )
Name(s) on Card	

Issued by	Card No.
Expiration Date	Lost Card Phone ( )
Name(s) on Card	

Issued by	Card No.
Expiration Date	Lost Card Phone ( )
Name(s) on Card	

Issued by	Card No.
Expiration Date	Lost Card Phone ( )
Name(s) on Card	

Three-hole punch and store any relevant information after this form.

C

Subscriptions

Include all magazines, newspapers and associations to which you subscribe. Include all business associations, clubs and fraternal organizations. Complete only those sections or forms that pertain to you.

Date Last Revised

Publication or Organization Name

Address

Date/s Payment Due   Amount Due $

Cancelation Phone (   )

Helpful Hint
It's important to keep a record of paid subscriptions in order to avoid double payment.

Publication or Organization Name

Address

Date/s Payment Due   Amount Due $

Cancelation Phone (   )

Publication or Organization Name

Address

Date/s Payment Due   Amount Due $

Cancelation Phone (   )

Publication or Organization Name

Address

Date/s Payment Due   Amount Due $

Cancelation Phone (   )

Publication or Organization Name

Address

Date/s Payment Due   Amount Due $

Cancelation Phone (   )

Publication or Organization Name

Address

Date/s Payment Due   Amount Due $

Cancelation Phone (   )

Three-hole punch and store any relevant information after this form.

Subscriptions

Continued

Publication or Organization Name

Address

Date/s Payment Due   Amount Due $

Cancelation Phone (   )

Publication or Organization Name

Address

Date/s Payment Due   Amount Due $

Cancelation Phone (   )

Publication or Organization Name

Address

Date/s Payment Due   Amount Due $

Cancelation Phone (   )

Publication or Organization Name

Address

Date/s Payment Due   Amount Due $

Cancelation Phone (   )

Publication or Organization Name

Address

Date/s Payment Due   Amount Due $

Cancelation Phone (   )

Publication or Organization Name

Address

Date/s Payment Due   Amount Due $

Cancelation Phone (   )

Three-hole punch and store any relevant information after this form.

Glossary

A–C

acquisition The procedure by which one company acquires, joins or buys another or takes over a controlling interest.

administrator A person who is appointed to carry out the court's decision regarding the disposition of assets of a deceased person who died without a will.

agent One that acts for or is representative of another in a transaction with a third party. For example, an insurance agent.

alternate date A date six months after a death that may be used for evaluating assets in an estate.

amortize The systematic reduction of debt by periodic payments of principal and interest, usually involving periodic payments of equal amounts covering principal and interest.

annual gift *See* gift.

annuitant One who receives the income from an annuity.

annuity A contract with an insurance company to provide a periodic income to an annuitant for a specific period of time, usually life. Such income may be paid monthly or quarterly.

annuity trust One form of charitable remainder trust that pays a fixed amount of income periodically according to the value of a gift at the time it is set up, age of donor and interest rates.

appraisal An expert valuation of something.

appraiser An expert who sets a value for real estate and valued assets.

appreciation The amount an item has increased in value over time.

asset A valuable item that is owned.

assignment To transfer the ownership rights of an insurance policy to another person, a trust or business entity.

ATM card A plastic device issued by financial institutions and used to access an automated teller machine to make deposits, transfer funds or obtain information or cash.

beneficiary The recipient of funds, property or other benefits from an insurance policy, will, living trust or other settlement.

bequest A gift of personal property through a will.

bond Certificate of debt issued by a government or corporation guaranteeing payment of the original investment plus interest by a specified future date. Good for long-term savings.

buy-sell agreement Agreement between partners defining the terms on which remaining partners may buy out the interest of a departing partner.

capital appreciation Price of the common stock share bought that appreciates or goes up.

capitalization The total value of owner's shares in a business firm; the outstanding stock or bonds in a corporation; the process of converting anticipated future income into present value.

cash-value insurance Life insurance that contains a savings account along with coverage for the life of the insured.

certificate of deposit (CD) A debt instrument issued by a financial institution which usually pays interest periodically. Maturities range from a few weeks to several years.

codicil An amendment or supplement to a will which adds to, subtracts from, qualifies, modifies or revokes provisions of a prior will.

commingling between married people Mixing of separate property with community property until specific portions can no longer be identified.

commingling in a professional or client relationship The mixing of the professional funds with those of the client. This is usually prohibited by law.

community property Property owned jointly by both husband and wife.

contingency An action that depends on something else happening, on conditions or events not yet established.

conveyance The act of transferring ownership from one person to another. This term can also refer to the instrument by which title is actually transferred.

correction deed Conveys title to property within a living trust when one person dies.

cost basis An asset's original cost. Used in determining depreciation and capital gains or losses. It is usually the purchase price; however, it could also be the market value at the time of the donor's death.

co-trustee A person who serves with another trustee in managing a living trust.

custodial account An account established by the parents of a minor for the purpose of overseeing the minor's assets.

custodian A person or financial institution that keeps custody of the property or assets of an individual, a mutual fund or another individual or corporate client.

D–G

death benefits Sum paid on life insurance policies, which includes all dividends and interest earned minus loans and interest accrued.

debit card Used like credit card but with direct line to cash accounts.

deed An instrument that conveys an interest in land from the grantor to the grantee.

devise The gift of real property by a will.

disability Condition or handicap that prevents an individual from working.

dividend Earnings and profits of a corporation paid to shareholders.

durable power of attorney A legal instrument that enables someone to act on the behalf of an individual who has suffered a physical or mental disability.

estate Everything that a person owns.

estate planning Planning how you want your estate handled in the event of your death. It should be updated every few years or whenever there is a significant change in your life.

estate taxes The amount due the government, usually based on the net value of one's property at death. Federal estate and gift taxes have been unified, meaning that one tabulation is kept for both kinds of events.

executor A person who is named in a will to carry out the instructions of the will.

exemption Amount allowed for each of the persons dependent upon a taxpayer's income, including himself, and deductible for income tax purposes.

fair market value A price agreed to between a buyer and a seller.

financial planner A professional who deals with your total financial picture and gives advice on investment, insurance, estate and tax planning.

gift The voluntary transfer of property. The liability for any taxes caused remains with the donor.

grantor One who executes a deed conveying title to property or creating a trust.

grantee The party to whom the title of real property is conveyed.

gross estate Total dollar value of both one's real and personal property.

group life insurance Life insurance provided at group rates, usually by an employer.

guardian A guardian is normally appointed by a court and is legally responsible for the care and upbringing of another person, usually a minor.

H–N

hard asset Property you own such as precious metals, gold, silver, gems and stamps.

heir A person who inherits by the terms of a will the assets of another.

holographic will A handwritten will.

inheritance tax A tax based on property value and imposed by a state on beneficiaries of estates.

interest The percentage rate charged for the use of money. The rate of return on an investment.

intestate The condition of having died without a will.

inventory A detailed list of possessions and their value.

investment brokerage An institution in business of investing another's money; stocks, mutual funds, money market funds, etc.

irrevocable Something that cannot be changed or canceled, as in a trust.

joint tenancy Property is owned by two or more tenants (owners) in equal shares. If one tenant dies, his or her share passes automatically to the other tenant(s).

JTWROS Joint tenancy with the rights of survivorship.

landlord One who owns property from whom one rents or leases.

liability An obligation or debt; when someone owes another something.

life interest A benefit, such as income from a trust, continuing for the life of the person holding the trust.

limited partnership A money-raising or investment device allowing partnership businesses to raise money without taking in new owners by selling partnership shares in the business.

living trust A trust that is a living document providing many advantages to you while you are living as well as after you die. It is set up to avoid probate and transfers all assets and property to the heirs per instructions at the time of death.

living will Your wishes expressed regarding life support and health care decisions.

marital deduction A deduction equal to half of an estate given to the surviving spouse at the time of death of a marriage partner.

market valuation Total cash value of all stocks available on the market.

maturity date Date on which bond issuer promises to return your money.

merger When companies merge or join, each company offers stock.

money market fund A mutual fund that invests primarily in government securities and bank certificates of deposit. These funds are managed by professionals and are usually invested in short-term instruments.

mortgage A temporary loan against property from a lending institution using that property as security.

mutual fund A large portfolio of common stocks, bonds, government securities, etc. managed by a professional manager.

net worth The total value of everything you own, minus any liabilities outstanding.

O–T

oral will A will given orally to a person, usually in the presence of witnesses. These wills are only recognized by a limited number of states.

personal property A tangible asset such as antiques, artwork, camera, clothing, computer, jewelry, etc.

prenuptial agreement A contract between a couple prior to marriage defining separate property.

probate court A court limited to the jurisdiction of probating wills and administering estates.

probate estate Property and assets distributed under direction of the probate court.

refinance Providing new financing in order to obtain a new and lower interest rate and payment schedule.

retirement funds The savings and investments you have set up for your retirement; 401(k), 403(b), IRA, etc.

right of survivorship If partners own something together, when one partner dies, his or her share passes automatically to the other.

safe deposit box A fire-proof metal box for safe storage of papers, jewelry or other valuables, located and rented from an institution.

secured credit card A credit card intended for people with a tarnished credit history or no history at all. Deposit the required amount of cash into a savings account, guarantee to keep the cash in the account for one year with a spending limit up to the amount in the account. The account holder will obtain interest on the account, at the same time establishing positive credit.

separate property Property kept separate from couple's joint property; owned separately.

settlement Payment of death benefits from life insurance to beneficiaries.

share A portion of ownership in a company; *see also* stock.

Social Security Measures by which the U. S. Government provides monetary assistance to persons faced with unemployment, disability or old age. The Social Security fund is financed by assessment of employers and employees. One is entitled to benefits if he or she is a worker, married to a worker or married to a worker 10 years or more.

statute of limitations A statute setting a time limit of enforcement of a right in certain cases.

stock A common stock is a share of a portion of ownership in a company.

stock split Change in the number of shares but does not change their capital value.

succession Series of heirs in line to receive inheritance.

supplemental insurance Secondary insurance paying deductibles, copayments, and some expenses not covered by the major insurance policy.

taxable estate The gross estate minus all debts, advisers' fees, court costs and taxes.

tax-saving trust Testamentary or living trust that segregates up to $600,000 of decedent's assets and places them in trust for all heirs.

tenancy in common Property owned by two or more tenants (owners) in equal or unequal shares. When one tenant dies, his or her share does not pass automatically to a spouse or other owner.

tenancy by the entirety Property owned in equal shares, cannot be sold without the consent of both spouses and, upon the death of one spouse, passes automatically to the surviving spouse.

term life insurance Insurance that is annually renewable and provides a death benefit only.

testate Having made a legally valid will before death.

title property Property with a title of ownership registered at a county agency, government office or with a company.

treasury bill (T-bills) A type of U. S. government bond purchased free from the Federal Reserve Bank or for a small fee through financial institutions.

trust A tool for transferring property to a trustee who will hold or manage the property for your beneficiary(s). This tool is used to avoid probate, minimize estate taxes, provide management of funds in the event of incapacitation and to protect dependents.

trust agreement A document setting out instructions for managing an estate left in a living trust.

trust estate The total value of property and assets transferred to the living trust by the trustor.

trustee A person or institution empowered to manage estate property.

trustor A person who establishes and funds a trust.

U–Z

Uniform Gifts to Minors Act (UGMA) A simplified trust agreement permitting a trustee to hold and manage assets for the benefit of minors.

Uniform Transfers to Minors Act (UTMA) Permits the ownership of real estate and other property not acceptable under UGMA.

whole life insurance Insurance that provides a death benefit as well as a cash investment.

will A document transferring property to successors through probate court. Without a will, it will greatly increase the cost of settling your estate and you may lose control over the disposition of your assets.

Index

Notes

Notes

Notes

Notes

Notes

Notes